HUGH PALMER WITH JAMES BENTLEY

The Most Beautiful Villages of the Loire

With 293 color illustrations

Thames & Hudson

Introduction

Best known for their grand châteaux, the beautiful villages of the Loire nevertheless display many more intimate delights, as at Crissay-sur-Manse (Indre-et-Loire) (above). In many places, the medieval street pattern still survives: a lane near the château of Sancerre (Cher) (opposite).

F RANCE'S LONGEST RIVER flows strong and wide through some of the richest regions of the country – rich in fertile countryside, but above all rich in history. From its mountain source hundreds of miles to the south in the Ardèche, the Loire weaves its way into the very heart of the country – into the ancient kingdom of Berry, right at its geographical centre.

Orléans, where the river swings west towards the Atlantic, was in medieval times the capital city, before Charles VII moved the royal court to Paris, one hundred kilometres to the north. Around Blois and Tours, a land of forests and vine-covered hills is divided by the Loire and its tributaries, the Cher, Indre, Vienne and Loir. Their valleys are studded with architectural wonders – châteaux built during the fifteenth and sixteenth centuries, when kings and their favoured courtiers poured huge fortunes into their architectural fantasies to display their (often transitory) wealth and power. As the river passes through the neighbouring dukedom of Anjou, older, more battle-worn châteaux look down from its banks, as it glides into the lands of Anjou's long-term enemy, the equally ancient kingdom of Brittany. And at Saint-Nazaire, a giant estuary sees the river meet the ocean, after a journey of more than six hundred miles.

The fertile plain watered by the Loire and its tributaries has long enjoyed the title of 'the garden of France', and almost everywhere the sight of vineyards, orchards and rich pastures welcomes the visitor. Even the areas where farming is less important, such as the wetlands of the Sologne, still provide a regular harvest for the hunter and the fisherman; and it was the plentiful deer and wild boar in the dense forests near Blois that attracted François I to the region, where he built his palatial château at Chambord. Produce from local market-gardens, stacked in such profusion in the village markets, underlies the strong regional traditions of the local cooking. The Loire still specializes in the production of *primeurs*, the early vegetables that appear two to three weeks before those cultivated around Paris: *asperges* and *haricots* from the Touraine, *oignons* and *échalotes* from Anjou, and *artichauts* from Angers – all are whisked up to the capital's markets and restaurants every spring, as they have been since trade in foodstuffs began.

Relics of past water-related industry abound in the Loire valley, like this giant wheel at a disused mill on the river Loir (opposite). In the village of Chenonceaux (Loir-et-Cher) (this page) such quiet corners provide a remarkable contrast to the grandeur of the château.

The vineyards of the Loire make up the fifth-largest wine-making region of France, and the *appellations* that stretch from Sancerre in the east to Muscadet in the west, cover such a range of styles, that only a very perverse peruser of a wine list is tempted to choose from outside the immediate locality. At present, just twelve per cent of the population are involved in agriculture of one sort or another, though this has never been a land of smoke-belching factories. Traditional occupations, better suited to the gentle flow of the river and the peaceful landscape, include such crafts as boat-building and rope-making. Other industries have created wealth in times past – the quarrying of limestone and of slate, the weaving of sailcloth – but these have disappeared, as have the fields of madder, hemp and liquorice, and the silkworm farms instituted by Louis XI. Happily, the activities that have recently replaced them have largely been countryside-friendly – hi-tech industries, insurance, banking and, above all, tourism. After all, it is the famous *douceur* of the land that attracts the visitors of today, as it would have given the first inhabitants reason to settle here millennia ago.

Those earliest residents have left behind plenty of souvenirs from their residence in the river's valley. In the west, especially, many groups of menhirs survive from the prehistoric age; at Saumur, the huge Bagneux dolmen, erected more than 5,000 years ago, is one of the most impressive Neolithic remains in Europe. The limestone of the area, which goes by the name of *tuffeau*, is soft and easily quarried – hence its transformation, in the hands of skilled masons, into the fantastic decorations of the Renaissance châteaux. The same qualities provided easy burrowing for the earliest inhabitants, whose cave-dwellings can still be seen. The Romans made use of the area's fertility during their largely peaceful occupation, after Julius Caesar's legions arrived in the first century B.C., when they are thought to have planted the first vines.

Christianity arrived in the region not long after Constantine declared it to be the religion of his empire. The celebrated and venerated bishop of Tours, St. Martin, was instrumental in encouraging its acceptance during the fourth century, and important centres of learning and culture flourished in monasteries at Angers, Orléans and Bourges. Meanwhile, feudal warlords fortified their strongholds against each other's attacks and commenced a long period of territorial disputes, which evolved into a bloody war between nations after Henri Plantagenet, Count of Anjou, inherited the English throne in 1154 as

In the département *of Loir-et-Cher, the visitor may be treated to the peace of rural life – at wood-encircled Lavardin* (above), *or to Baroque splendour – here, in the form of the Jesuit church of Saint-Vincent, Blois* (opposite).

Henry II. Many of the harshest campaigns of the Hundred Years War were fought along the Loire, and it was at Orléans that Jeanne d'Arc finally helped to turn the tide in the favour of her beloved France. More fighting was to come: the persecution of the Protestant Huguenots during the Wars of Religion and, after the Revolution, the loyalists of the Vendée in the west suffered brutal reprisals after their insurrection. In between all this bloodshed, however, kings and nobles were building wonderful châteaux and endowing the towns and villages under their protection with stone-built mansions and fine churches. Even after the royal courts had returned to Paris, the region stayed prosperous, with the Loire itself forming the most important trade route in the country, to be eclipsed only in the nineteenth century by the arrival of the railways.

Now the region still benefits from its geographical position and its proximity to the capital, although it is a trade that comes from all over the world that forms the basis of its continuing prosperity: the constant flow of visitors who come to marvel at the historical treasures and to relax in the enchanting countryside.

Around Orléans

ORLÉANS MARKS THE NORTHERNMOST point of the Loire's six-hundred-mile journey from its mountain source to the Atlantic. To the south lies the ancient dukedom of Berry, still wooded and enclosed; here, among the quiet villages that epitomize *La France profonde*, several candidates bicker amiably over which should bear the distinction of marking the exact geographical centre of the country. The Loire forms an important divide to the east of the region, separating it from the kingdom of Burgundy, as it passes by the rich vineyards of Sancerre, overlooked by Sancerre itself, from its commanding hill-top.

By the time it reaches Orléans itself the river is already of the greatest strategic importance. It was here that the fervent patriot Jeanne d'Arc, a country girl from Lorraine, stirred the flagging resistance of the beleaguered Orléanais, and turned the tide of the Hundred Years War against the invading English. Further downstream, where the river forms a natural defence against attack from the north, the castles and bridges have been witnesses to strategic battles at every era from medieval times until the last World War.

While the north banks of the river have offered shelter and protection in medieval times, they now provided ideal growing conditions for vines on the south-facing slopes. South of the river, the flat alluvial flood-plain provides wonderful soil for the successful growing of vegetables and fruit, while the scrubby woodland gives way to the denser forests to the west, where generations of kings and courtiers came to hunt.

The vineyards of the Sancerre area, planted with the Sauvignon Blanc grape, cluster around their individual villages, as at Sury-en-Vaux (Cher), seen here from the south-east.

Apremont-sur-Allier

CHER

ON A MAP, the river Allier may not look very impressive, a mere tributary of the Loire, which it joins just six kilometres north of Apremont. The visitor will be surprised, therefore, to find a wide-flowing, stately river, which contrasts pleasantly with the decidedly rustic settlement on its western bank. The only building to match its noble bearing is the ancient château, which stands on a hill at the southern edge of the village. Its comfortable-looking main wing gives it the air of a classic *demeure d'agrément,* as it had indeed become by the beginning of the nineteenth century, for the summer use of the Marquis de Saint-Saveur, who had married into the family. But behind the elegant façade stand five fortified towers and the remains of a curtain wall – testament to a less tranquil period in its history. Indeed, before the beginning of the Hundred Years War it was reported to have a total of fourteen towers to help defend what must have been an important stronghold. Most of it was nevertheless destroyed during the incessant fighting that followed.

A happier event in Apremont's history occurred in 1894, when the successor to the female line married local industrialist Eugène Schneider. He made it his life's work to beautify not only the castle and its grounds, but also the village, skilfully editing out any modern buildings and rebuilding them in the medieval style of the region. His efforts, and the obvious pride of the residents, give the village a harmonious charm, much helped by the tranquillity of its setting. The stone from which its houses are built comes from the many local quarries, which accounted for the ancient prosperity of the place. Flat-bottomed barges laden with *tuffeau,* the limestone of the district, were floated down to supply the huge ecclesiastical construction projects at Orléans and Saint-Benoît. In the beautifying tradition of Schneider, his grandson, Gilles de Brissac, laid out a notable *parc floral* in the English style, with many picturesque follies artfully distributed among its trees and lakes.

The grand seventeenth-century wing of Apremont's château dominates the more prosaic dwellings of this river-bank village.

The apparently well-preserved nature of many of the village's older houses is in fact a pleasant illusion (these pages). Most of them were substantially reconstructed at the end of the nineteenth century by the enlightened industrialist, Eugène Schneider.

*I*n the shadow of the castle, a picturesque parc floral *has been laid out in the 'English style', complete with the oriental features so admired by English designers of the late eighteenth and early nineteenth centuries.*

Aubigny-sur-Nère
CHER

A complex maze of winding streets and steeply raked roofs makes up the centre of the old village, notable especially for its wealth of sixteenth-century timbered houses (these pages).

AUBIGNY has the air of a prosperous community; its prosperity is largely owed to a long and unusual association with the Stuart clan of Scotland. It was Charles VII who chose to reward Sir John Stuart of Darnley, for his help in defeating the English forces at Baugé in 1421. He gave Sir John a substantial estate around the village of Aubigny itself, as well as land further to the east, where his son Béraud Stuart started the construction of the lakeside Château de la Verrerie. The Stuart family continued to serve their French allies, adding their troops and generalship to support the campaigns of the French kings: Sir John's nephew Robert accompanied François I on his Italian campaigns, whence he returned to add a stylish *loggia* to La Verrerie. He also had enough resources and

continued enthusiasm for building to step in when a devastating fire destroyed almost all of Aubigny in 1512. Many of the wonderful old timbered houses in the centre of the village date from the years immediately after the fire.

It is a rewarding village to explore, almost every turn of the narrow old streets giving a new glimpse of a sixteenth-century half-timbered house. As well as a circular defensive wall, with four fortified gates, the village was also protected by water, with the Nère widened to make a lake to the south, and another stream (the Ruisseau des Échanges) diverted to run around the walls. Some of the battlements to the north still survive, and much of the Ruisseau, crossed by little bridges from Le Mail

Guichard. In the east of the village, where the Stuarts rebuilt the château in the sixteenth century, no evidence of fortifications remain: a broad street leads out towards the peaceful castle gardens, laid out a hundred years later by a pupil of Le Nôtre. Inside the château, which was modernized towards the end of the seventeenth century by Louise de Kéroualle, Duchess of Portsmouth, the *mairie* shares the accommodation with some historical displays, including a small *musée* commemorating the 'Auld Alliance'. Indeed, the Franco-Scottish connection had a particularly long history here; in the eighteenth century, refugees from the Jacobite terror made their way to Aubigny and settled.

The Gothic church of Saint-Martin (top) *contains a number of treasures, including this sumptuously decorated statue* (above). *Dominating the village, though, is the sixteenth-century Château des Stuarts, a powerful reminder of the 'Auld Alliance' of Scots and French* (opposite). *On a more domestic scale is a fanciful* belle époque *addition to a much older merchant's house in the village centre* (right).

La Chapelle-d'Angillon
CHER

EARLY-FLOWERING literary genius, a life cut off before its prime: such elements can easily become a legend. This was the story of Henri Alain-Fournier, born in this village on 3 October 1886, and many visitors still make the pilgrimage to no. 35 Avénue Alain-Fournier to read the simple plaque that denotes his birthplace. In his celebrated novel,

*T*he sound of the old mill-race is almost the only disruption to the peace of the streets around the village church (these pages).

*I*t is impossible to distance oneself far from water in La Chapelle-d'Angillon. One of its rivulets, the Petite Sauldre (above), flows past the local church; the village's château (right) *looms over its former moat, now expanded into a fishing lake.*

Le Grand Meaulnes, he created a magical world of rural tranquillity, based on the lovely countryside that surrounds 'La Ferté d'Angillon', as he playfully re-christened his home village. The novel was published in 1913 – a year later its author was lying among the countless French dead on the Western Front.

The eleventh-century château, which includes a lively Musée Alain-Fournier, has an equally romantic link with its more ancient past: it was the home, during the fifteenth century, of Marie d'Albret, Duchesse de Clèves. It was she who is supposed to have inspired the heroine's character in the first novel written in the French language, *La Princesse de Clèves*. In real life, she presided with her husband Charles over the principality of Boisbelle which, despite its tiny size, had the distinction of owing allegiance to no monarch. The well-defended château is a moated quadrilateral affair.

La Ferté-Saint-Aubin
LOIRET

THE SOLOGNE, that huge area of marsh and
wetland lying between the Loire and the Cher,
is today a place of pilgrimage for nature-lovers,
bird-watchers and, in the autumn, hunters after
waterfowl. In the past, it provided meagre
sustenance for its peasantry. We find in the records
of local tradespeople references to a mixture of
fishing, wood-felling, livestock-breeding and
wine-making, with a fair number involved in
the textile and weaving trade. After the railway
arrived in 1846, the population rose swiftly, as
several manufactories and a foundry were opened.
Now the industry has all but departed, and again
it is the Sologne that has to sustain the village.

The fine château from which the village takes
its name (*ferté* is an old French word meaning

'stronghold') stands by the banks of the Cosson, close to where a fortified *péage* is mentioned in the records for 1139. The main buildings, presenting a grand symmetrical façade across the *parc* to the west, date from the mid seventeenth century. The approach is grand indeed – the visitor crosses a wide moat, enters beneath a pedimented *portail* between twin pavilions, giving on to a huge courtyard, itself flanked by symmetrical stable wings, also on a huge scale. The château, whose façade is now revealed, turns out to be rather charmingly asymmetrical, with a relatively modest sixteenth-century *petit-château*, with its original brickwork, growing, like a graph of the family's rising fortunes, into a distinctly palatial *grand-château*, complete with lavishly decorated windows on its second floor. The family in question was that of de Saint-Nectaire, whose third-generation Henri, after numerous successful campaigns, rose to be a Marshal of France during the reign of King Louis XIII.

Preceding pages
*T*he old parts of the village are dominated by the château (left *and* above)*, built over a long period in the sixteenth and seventeenth centuries.*

*T*he approach to the château is flanked by two grand blocks (below)*; the use of one is denoted by a terracotta horse's head positioned above its entrance* (left).

A number of the apartments and galleries of the château (left), decorated in a variety of historical styles, are open to the public.

E xtensive redecoration of the stables and saddlery (above and right) has uncovered a wealth of original fittings and equipment.

*I*n the oldest quartier *of the village,*
by the church of Saint-Martin
(these pages), *a substantial number*
of ancient half-timbered houses are
enthusiastically maintained by their
present owners.

Almost every viewpoint in Mehun yields something of interest and visual excitement: an old wash-house by the banks of one of the many tributaries of the Yèvre (left); looking through the Porte de l'Horloge down the Rue Jeanne d'Arc (below); the main tower of the collegiate church of Notre-Dame, viewed from the Jardins du Duc de Berry (opposite).

Mehun-sur-Yèvre

CHER

THE NEATLY fortified village of Mehun sits on a rocky spur which commands the tranquil water-meadows of the Yèvre. In 1366, a newly arrived *seigneur* started to add to the existing twelfth-century keep on its southern tip. Jean, Duc de Berry, was vying with his brothers, the dukes of neighbouring Anjou and Burgundy, in the creation of a courtly lifestyle of exceptional opulence. Although his seat of government was at Bourges, his real joy was his château at Mehun, and it is no surprise to find representations of it, idealized but very recognizable, in *Les Très Riches Heures du Duc de Berry*.

At his death, the dukedom passed to his great-nephew Charles, the twelve-year-old Dauphin, who came to Mehun in 1417, and was proclaimed King Charles VII five years later in the château's chapel. Jeanne d'Arc came here after her heroic campaign against the English during the year of 1429, and was ennobled by her king on 29 December, a few paces away from where her statue now stands in the Place du Château. Charles, criticized by some for abandoning Jeanne to her fate at Rouen the next year, certainly enjoyed the court life that flourished again once the war had ended. His arrival here was to usher in a century of royal interest in the Loire, although after his own death here in 1461, the focus soon moved westwards, with the establishment of Louis XI's court at Tours.

A statue of Joan of Arc, who once wintered in the village, stands next to the eleventh-century collegiate church, surmounted by a thirteenth-century tower (this page). *The* donjon (opposite) *was originally built in 1196, then later given its machicolated extension during the Renaissance period.*

Meung-sur-Loire

LOIRET

THE OLDER part of Meung-sur-Loire manages to hide itself away from the busy N152, which makes its way west from Orléans along the north bank of the Loire. A descent towards the river down narrow, ancient streets brings the visitor eventually to the quiet main square. The huge church there seems at first too grand for the village, a modest place built on the proceeds of its vineyards (now defunct), its riverside warehouses, and the watermills that used to line the various channels of Les Mauves, the stream which runs down to the Loire. The history of the Collégiale Saint-Liphard soon makes clear that it was built on this scale as part of an abbey.

The ecclesiastical status of the village was emphatically retained even after the abbey itself had disappeared, for from the twelfth century onwards the château became the episcopal residence for the Bishops of Orléans, and remained so until the Revolution. The bishops were allowed to administer justice in their diocese, but since episcopal law did not allow for the execution of their convicts, frequent use was made of the gaol, in which prisoners could be left to starve to death - a more 'natural' though undoubtedly less humane end. The raffish poet François Villon ended up here in 1461, after his arrest for stealing a gold chalice from the church at nearby Baccon. With his customary good luck, Villon became one of the few to emerge alive from his imprisonment. He was pardoned by Louis XI, a frequent visitor.

The collegiate church of Saint-Liphard rises above the outbuildings of the château, formerly an official residence of the Bishops of Orléans (far left).

The old village centre, notable for some fine half-timbered buildings (left) *is dissected by numerous waterways (Les Mauves) which flow down to the Loire* (below).

Rather than execute their prisoners, the ecclesiastical masters of the château caused them to be lowered by ropes into an underground oubliette (left *and* far left), *where they usually died of starvation or illness.*

The château of Meung, restored by the present owner (above), *is a mixture of styles* (opposite), *from the medieval to sixteenth- and seventeenth-century. Its interior, however, was largely remodelled in the nineteenth century* (right).

Cathedrals and Churches

THE GREAT EVANGELIZING bishop of Tours, St. Martin, was said to have brought three vines with him from his native Hungary. Whether or not the introduction of wine-making to the Touraine may be added to his other miraculous workings, the extraordinary spread of the Christian faith during his life (he died at Candes in 397) cannot be doubted. Many of the earlier village churches, displaying the engagingly unadorned style of the Romanesque, were originally attached to monasteries or abbeys. Good examples are the lofty collegiate churches at Saint-Aignan and Selles-sur-Cher, left rather high and dry without their abbeys, which were pulled down by zealous Republicans after the Revolution. One extraordinary survival remains to give us an idea of the extent and grandeur of these monastic complexes - the great abbey of Fontevraud, south of Saumur.

Sometimes the very modesty of a village has preserved the simplicity of its church. The riverside hamlet of Chenillé-Changé has just such a treasure - the peacefulness of its setting in the tiny village square gives the impression that new fashions in architecture simply passed it by. Of similar age is the quirky cluster of village churches around Baugé, also of simple Romanesque form, but topped with distinctively twisted spires. A more practical building fashion also originated from Anjou, the 'Angevin vault', a domed system of vaulted ceilings that allowed for yet more height – as in the dizzying nave at Candes-Saint-Martin. This style spread as far as Italy, an important precursor to the glories of full-blown Gothic, which is expressed in its ultimate, some would say least digestible form on the west front of the cathedral of Saint-Gatien at Tours. The interior is fascinating to explore: an intricate ensemble of different styles and periods (building works continued over three hundred years), soaring up to the great rose-windows dating from the twelfth century, some depicting the colourful career of St. Martin himself.

Always architecturally fascinating, the churches of the Loire valley come in many shapes, sizes and periods: twelfth-century simplicity at Chenillé-Changé (Maine-et-Loire) (opposite); the elaborate pile of Saint-Florent-le-Vieil opposite La Meilleraie (Loire-Atlantique) (right).

*T*he area around Baugé, the Pays Baugeois
(Maine-et-Loire), is famous for its churches
with strangely twisted spires; one of the most notable
is that of Saint-Denis at Pontigné (below), and there
are others at Mouliherne (below left) and at Le
Guedeniau (bottom right). Further east, the priory
of Lavardin (Loir-et-Cher) has a splendidly sculpted
interior (left).

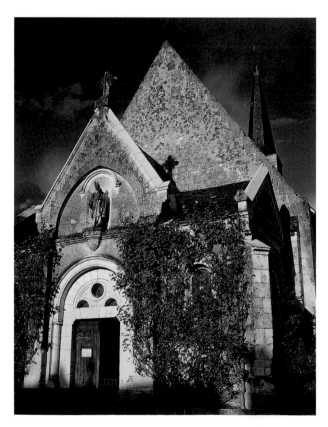

The collegiate church of Saint-Ours in Loches (Indre-et-Loire) (exterior and interior below) has two octagonal pyramids between its towers, a form reflected in the twelfth-century vaulting of the nave.

The façade of Saint-Laud at Angers makes a spectacular sight at evening time (above), viewed here from the Place du Président-Kennedy, on the edge of the old town.

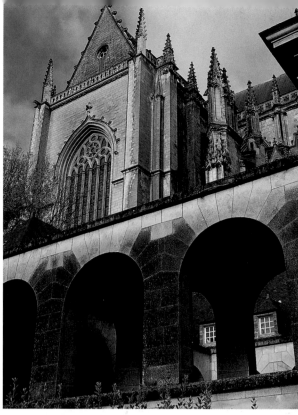

*S*plendours of the Loire cathedrals: that of Saint-
Gatien at Tours is a remarkable mixture of
styles (opposite), *being Romanesque at its base,
Flamboyant Gothic on the main façade, with the
two towers topped off in a Renaissance style. The
fourteenth-century stained-glass in the transept
(below) and elsewhere is of great beauty.*

*T*he south transept of the cathedral of
Nantes, dedicated to Saints Peter and
Paul, contains the finely sculpted tomb of
François II (above *and* top).

From every angle the cathedral of Saint-Étienne at Bourges attracts the eye: flying buttresses and clerestory windows at the east end (opposite), and medieval carving around the mighty south door (below).

Sainte-Croix, the cathedral of Orléans (above), is another arresting mixture of styles; its origins were in the thirteenth century, although building continued until the sixteenth. After its partial destruction in that century, it was later rebuilt in Gothic style, a process lasting until the nineteenth century. The early eighteenth-century woodwork of the choir-stalls in the chancel (right) was carried out to designs by Mansart, Gabriel and Lebrun.

Around Blois and Tours

BOTH LOUIS XII, at the end of the fifteenth century, and his successor François I poured huge resources into the establishment of a royal court at Blois and spent much of their reigns there. François went on to build the colossal château at Chambord in the forest that was the chief hunting preserve of his court. Dominating French political and artistic life for more than a century, the region benefited greatly from the wave of creativity and innovation that the French kings brought back from their campaigning in Italy. The changing architectural styles of the sixteenth and seventeenth centuries are reflected in the great châteaux clustered around Blois and Tours, and their richness and importance are reflected in the villages that were built under their protection.

Fine stone houses and public buildings, as well as the splendid churches, demonstrate the distribution of wealth outside the castle walls. Even remote villages such as Crissay-sur-Manse, whose feudal lord was an absentee who never stayed long enough to complete his château, can boast some superb architecture; the vineyards and rolling farmland surrounding the village were obviously rich enough to subsidize the pretensions of the local bourgeoisie. The wines of the Touraine, which include famous names such as Bourgeuil, Chinon and Vouvray, have a long history; the first mention of post-Roman cultivation of vines on the banks of the Loire goes back to the year 550. It is no coincidence that this production was from the earliest times centred on Tours. Ever since the times of its first bishops, St. Gatien and St. Martin, and the foundation of monasteries throughout the region, monks were instrumental in recording and transmitting the art of making wine, as well as taking a financial interest in its popularity.

Two noble architectural profiles dominate the Cher at Saint-Aignan: the Renaissance wing of the château, home of the Beauvilliers family, and the twin towers of the collegiate church.

Azay-le-Rideau
INDRE-ET-LOIRE

F amous principally for its gem of a château, the village of Azay itself displays an elegant prosperity, originally based on the activities of the numerous mills which once lined the river Indre (above and opposite).

THE NOVELIST Balzac, who spent much of his life at nearby Saché, described the château at Azay-le-Rideau as resembling 'a many-faceted diamond, set in the Indre'. The elegance of this Renaissance jewel, glimpsed through trees as it sits demurely on its own island, does exert an almost feminine charm. Indeed, tradition has it that although wealthy financier Gilles Berthelot commissioned the building in the early sixteenth century, it was his wife, Philippa Lesbahy, who actually supervised its design and construction. Since then, the centuries have done little to dull the château's beauty; the extension of the moat to form a small, reflecting lake has given it further opportunity to show off its charms.

The pretensions of Berthelot were short-lived, however, and the château was not yet completed when in 1527 his fortunes changed abruptly. Whether for reasons of his own guilt, or by association with the misdemeanours of fellow financier Jacques de Beaune-Semblançay, who was executed at Montfaucon, Berthelot fled his

home and his country, to die in exile abroad. François I duly confiscated the château and presented it to a favourite named Antoine Raffin. Rather like a valuable but unlucky jewel, the château at Azay-le-Rideau passed through many hands in the centuries that followed, to be bought finally by the State in 1905, for the sum of 200,000 francs. The most distinctive feature of the château is the great staircase, with its storeys of twin bays crowned by a large sculpted pediment. Inside, there is fine furniture from the seventeenth century and an extensive collection of tapestries.

The village itself can hardly be said to be dominated by its famous château, which hides itself so coyly behind a screen of trees. Indeed, its houses have a grand air in their own right, many of them oriented towards the Indre, which is divided into numerous mill-races below the bridge. Further evidence of the prosperity of the village is in the local wine production – the present vineyards under the *appellation* of Azay-le-Rideau cover over 100 acres, producing white and rosé wines.

*The well-maintained houses which contribute
so much to Azay's air of well-being
(opposite* and *left) date from many periods.*

Other corners of the village (above) *have a
distinctly rustic air, while the waterside
location contributes hugely to the charm of the
village and its château* (right).

The village and the great house (these pages); veteran saddler, Monsieur Poiret (right), is no stranger to the stables of the château (left); one of the latter's most prominent features is the grand staircase (opposite).

Candes-Saint-Martin

INDRE-ET-LOIRE

A fascinating complex of old lanes and alleys, the village stands on the site of a former river port at the confluence of the rivers Vienne and Loire (these pages).

THE SITE of Candes-Saint-Martin, its houses clustered tightly on a steep limestone bank above the fast-flowing Vienne, suggests that its earliest inhabitants would have looked to river traffic as a natural means of livelihood. The village looks down directly on to the confluence of the Vienne, running down from Chinon, and the Loire, on its way from Amboise. Thus was established an important staging post for goods and passengers, as well as a busy ferry point. The Rue des Mariniers, the Rue des Pêcheurs and the Rue du Port all bear witness to a past of vigorous river life. The remains of the once-bustling quays have all but disappeared, but it is pleasant to explore the little cobbled *ruelles* that run down to the river from the main street.

The other main distinction of Candes, however, has left a more enduring monument: the collegiate church of Saint-Martin, dedicated to the soldier-turned-bishop who founded a priory, school and chapel here, which he dedicated to fellow-soldier St. Maurice. After Martin died here on a visit from Tours in 397, his reputation was such that his place of death became a place of pilgrimage, and the present church reflects that importance. The entrance porch, with its gothic vaulting supported by a single, graceful pillar, unusually faces north, towards the river where the pilgrims would have disembarked. Most of the many carved figures around the doorway were defaced or decapitated after the Wars of Religion; inside the church, however, some delightful groups depicting Noah, Daniel and other biblical adventurers, escaped a similar fate, protected by their inviolable position on top of the pillars that support the magnificent lofty chancel arch.

*O*ld-style river craft may still be seen on the Vienne by the old river port (left). *The original church of the village, which still has some exquisitely pretty corners (opposite), was built on the place where Saint Martin died in 397. The present building (below) was completed in the thirteenth century and given its rather military aspect in the fifteenth.*

*T*he gardens of the château *(these pages), formerly the summer residence of the Bishops of Tours, yield superb views of the Vienne and the Loire. One unusual feature is what appears to be an animal-baiting pit* (opposite).

The supporting village of Chambord (these pages) is entirely dominated by the phantasmagorical towers of the palatial château.

Chambord
LOIR-ET-CHER

HOWEVER well-prepared the visitor may be for the grandeur of Chambord, it is still a shock to emerge from dense forest to see the château sitting in its huge clearing, like a gigantic version of a fairytale cottage in a magic glade. Its history has a touch of madness about it; visitors have always come to look at it as much as a curiosity as an outstanding work of art.

Sixty years before, the newly crowned François I was already lavishing huge sums on his stylish Italianate improvements to the royal base at Blois. By 1518, when work began at Chambord, he was already showing signs of the spending addiction that would push him and his kingdom perilously close to bankruptcy throughout his reign. He was already planning a huge château to replace that of Romorantin, his boyhood home. Plans had been drawn up by Leonardo da Vinci, who in his old age had been brought back to Amboise by François after his Italian campaign – cultural booty in its ultimate form. An outbreak of plague at Romorantin robbed that town of its chance of a more glorious place in history. Shortly afterwards, the king started work at Chambord.

Construction was to continue for almost all of the remaining thirty years of his life, but François' enthusiasm for the project never waned. Even when his sons were held captive in Spain, languishing there for want of a ransom, money continued to be poured into the works at Chambord. The grandness of François' vision was really in anticipating the great architectural statements of royal power and prestige that reached their zenith in Versailles. By 1527, he was proposing that the river Loire itself should be bent, literally, to his royal will, and be diverted to flow in front of the château. The smaller Cosson, which had the advantage of being on the spot instead of five kilometres to the north, was eventually chosen.

Even a 440-room miniature city needed to have its suburbs, and to house some of the host of retainers necessary to staff the place (even for the infrequent occasions when it was ever used), a small village grew up, comprising estate houses, a *mairie*, a church and even some farm buildings and cottages, whose rustic simplicity sets off the stunning grandeur of the château itself.

Chambord's château is truly a city in one house (left); its every feature is full of drama and history – as the double staircase (top) and the royal apartments (above) show.

Cheverny

LOIR-ET-CHER

SEPARATED from each other by the waters of the
little river Conon, the two villages of Cheverny and
Cour-Cheverny huddle at the north-western edge
of the Sologne. This area of lakes and forests has a
long tradition of hunting - hence the location near
here of Chambord, François I's favourite hunting
lodge. Vines flourish here too: both villages boast
an *appellation controlée*. Cour-Cheverny's was
granted as recently as 1993, for the production of
an idiosyncratic white wine made from the local
Romorantin grape.

Cheverny has its famous château; over the
bridge, Cour-Cheverny has the more substantial
houses, a street of shops, and a little sheltered
square beside the church of Saint-Agnan. The
medieval scale of the streets, often running between
ancient houses with stonework worn and mellowed
over the centuries, are a suitable *amuse-gueule*
before the main course is proudly displayed – the
immaculate seventeenth-century façade of the
rebuilt château. The whole confection dazzles the
viewer in a literal sense; the *tuffeau* of the building,
quarried locally at Bourré, is said to grow whiter
and harder as it ages, and this unlikely-sounding
claim seems to be borne out here in full.
Constructed in a single time-span between 1620
and 1634, the château's design, by Jacques Bougier,
the architect of Blois, is completely of the
seventeenth century.

If folklore is to be believed, Count Henri
Hurault, who commissioned the new château, had
good reason to efface any memories of his former
dwelling. He is said to have killed his first wife and
her lover here, returning hotfoot from the Parisian
court, where he had overheard rumours of his
cuckoldry. With his second wife, he certainly
spared no expense on every detail of the interior;
there are wall-paintings by Jean Mosnier and, in a
separate wing, a magnificent state bedroom whose
bed is canopied with embroidered silk from Persia.

The famous façade, used by *Tintin* illustrator
and author Hergé as the model for Captain
Haddock's Moulinsart, is an entirely appropriate
backdrop for the equally famous pack of hounds,
which still runs out twice weekly during the season,
to the trumpeting of the great curled hunting horns
of the period.

*D*azzling tufa stone from Bourré gives the
south front of the château an illusory
appearance of newness (opposite). The royal
apartments – a required feature in all large
châteaux – have a particularly sumptuous bed,
canopied with embroidered Persian silk (above).

*A*s in many Loire villages, the rustic simplicity
of Cheverny's centre (this page) is in stark
contrast to the grandeur of the château.

In spite of the simplicity of many village dwellings (this page), *there is clearly an immense pride in their appearance and upkeep.*

Crissay-sur-Manse

INDRE-ET-LOIRE

FROM its retired position on a hillside overlooking farmlands of the Manse valley, Crissay could, in centuries past, have justifiably envied the strategic siting of other fortified villages in the area. Its own castle was developed gradually over five centuries after the domain became the fief of Guillaume de Turpin and his heirs. Through several generations they held the office of Royal Chamberlain at the court of Anjou. A Jacques Turpin accompanied his king, François I, on his Italian campaigns. He returned, like his monarch, with a taste for the new Italian Renaissance architecture, and started building a residence according to the new fashion. It was never finished nor inhabited and stands among the remains of the earlier eleventh- and twelfth-century fortress. While other communities in the region were devastated by the tides of war,

Crissay was largely left untouched. Now, with its tiny population of just over 100, the village seems to have reaped the benefits of its obscurity. The pristine condition of many of its buildings perfectly matches the tranquillity of its setting. A wonderful collection of houses cluster around its Place Haute, displaying finely mullioned windows and decorated dormers.

Apart from agriculture, industry is a low-key affair here, typified in the small *laboratoire* set up in the Rue du Château, where Monsieur Laubigeau, the local *apiculteur*, devises ever more delicious ways of using the honey from his hives, which are spread widely about the neighbouring countryside. His *marmelade de citron*, containing lemon peel marinated in honey, is a particular *tour de force*.

*T*he main village of Crissay-sur-Manse (these pages) *looks especially enticing when seen across the surrounding countryside. Well-kept houses and gardens express its innate prosperity.*

A number of the village houses have been carefully restored and the whole is quite remarkable for the neat charm of its appearance (these pages).

*T*he château of Crissay-sur-Manse was intended to be a Renaissance palazzo, inspired by the original owner's visits to Italy with François I. It was never finished and still remains a ruin amid the remains of an earlier medieval edifice (left *and* below).

The rather grand houses of the village centre (this page) are themselves dwarfed by the massive entry keep of the castle (opposite) and the forbidding walls and towers (overleaf); even the apartments seem scarcely on a human scale.

Langeais
INDRE-ET-LOIRE

EARLY attempts to bridge the Loire at Langeais proved too ambitious. The river is wide and strong here, and its winter floods swept away several versions before the present suspension bridge was completed in 1951; its four massive concrete piles echo the equally hefty entrance to Langeais' castle.

Doughty defensiveness was certainly a major theme, if not a necessity, when the château was built in the middle of the fifteenth century; its feudal character is emphasized by its huge entrance towers, augmented by a drawbridge that is still in action. The private face of the château, dating from the second half of the fifteenth century, is a great contrast. Its elegant Renaissance façade looks quietly out over to the formal gardens and also on to the remains of the first castle keep, a war-scarred relic of the times of its builder, Foulques Nerra, Count of Anjou, known as the Black Falcon.

Inside the spacious castle is a sequence of splendidly decorated chambers. Many of them are furnished with the rare fifteenth- and sixteenth-century tapestries that were acquired by the wealthy and impassioned collector Jacques Siegfried who, in the late nineteenth century, devoted much of his life to restoring Langeais to its present glorious state of preservation.

Lavardin

LOIR-ET-CHER

MORE THAN half of Lavardin's château was pulled down by the order of Henri IV, whose soldiers were the last force to besiege it in 1589. Nonetheless, it still presents an impressive aspect to today's visitor, especially when approached across the eight-arched gothic bridge over the Loir, from the neighbouring village of Montoire. The gatehouse and the massive keep still give an idea of its impregnability, especially in the days when it was protected by three sets of encircling walls. Lavardin's strategic position, on the border between the Capetian and Angevin kingdoms, meant that it was constantly under attack during the bitter struggles between the Plantagenets and the French kings. In 1188, almost exactly four hundred years before Henri IV's *coup de grace*, both Henry II and Richard the Lionheart attempted to storm the fortress, but in vain.

The view from the château's ramparts looks over the old stone houses of the village, squeezed between the Loir and the limestone bank that borders the river. Many wine-cellars and even more dwellings have been burrowed out of the soft *tuffeau* over the years, and these can be explored

The main street of the village (above) passes by the priory church of Saint-Genest, the main building in view from the ruins of the castle ramparts (left).

83

Lavardin is joined to its neighbour, Montoire, by this bridge (left). *Gardens on the Grande Rue and elegant houses on the Rue de la Barrière* (below *and* opposite) *make the centre a particularly delightful place.*

along a leafy path which offers fine views of the valley below. Standing pre-eminent in the view from the château, though, is the Prieuré Saint-Genest, almost all that remains of two priories that once flourished in the village. The present *mairie* occupies the old priory, with some fine old rooms dating from the twelfth century. The church's fortified exterior presents a robust face to the world; a square bell-tower has replaced a stone spire destroyed by lightning. A treasure trove of mural paintings illuminates its simple Romanesque interior. The earliest, dating from the twelfth century, feature astrological symbols alongside depictions of the life of Christ.

No series of views of a French village would be complete without one of a potager, *a kitchen garden (below), one of a number of engaging backyard details in Lavardin (right).*

The architecture of the collegiate church of Saint-Sylvain (below *and* right) *and the massive Porte de Champagne* (opposite) *seems grandiose for such a small community.*

Levroux

INDRE

ENRICHED by the forests and rich farmland (La Champagne Berrichonne) that surround it, Levroux was well enough established in medieval times to have built up a good stock of fine timbered houses, many of which survive today. The narrow streets of the old village centre lead to the commanding Collégiale Saint-Sylvain and, in its shadow, the finest of the medieval houses, the Maison de Bois. Its first floor projects dramatically over the street, designed to shelter the entrance below, as well as gain extra space above. The timber corbelling is richly decorated with carvings in the gothic style, unlike the almost classical shape of the pillars beside the doors, which look forward to the Renaissance influence. Today, the Maison de Bois houses the tourist office, suitably enough, since its alternative name, Maison Saint-Jacques, looks back to a long established tradition of welcoming pilgrims en route to the shrine of St. James of Compostela.

Built in the thirteenth century, the village church was attached to a college of canons, founded two hundred years earlier and dedicated to St. Sylvain. Pilgrims made their way here to pray for relief from the skin complaint that bears his name, *feu Saint-Sylvain*, an echo of another role of this village in earlier times, that of a haven for lepers. Indeed, the name of the village is thought to be a corruption of *vicus leprosus*.

A proclamation of 15 January 1436, issued by Charles VII, allowed the inhabitants of Levroux to

*T*he finest medieval house in Levroux is the fabulously decorated Maison de Bois (above and opposite). Equally well-endowed is the church of Saint-Sylvain (right and right above), with its fine fifteenth-century organ.

raise taxes to pay for its fortification. A particularly massive gate was built to defend the southern approaches, the Porte de Champagne, which still exists in splendid order today. Formerly, defensive walls encircled the entire village, but only fragments now survive. In later, more peaceful times, the villagers developed their skills in the crafts of leather-curing and the manufacture of parchment. Another local activity is the production of a goat's cheese in the shape of a pyramid, modelled perhaps on the distinctive profile of the collegiate church's bell-tower.

Montrésor

INDRE-ET-LOIRE

MONTRÉSOR is small and grand at the same time, and still has the air of being as rich as its name suggests. Eleven hundred years ago, it was the property of the wealthy Treasurer of the Diocese of Tours. Lying on the borders of the kingdom of Touraine, it was important enough strategically to catch the eye of the Count of Anjou, Foulques Nerra. He built a fortress on top of a hill, overlooking the now tranquil Indrois valley. The twin entrance towers were added in the twelfth century. In 1493 the Bastarnay family acquired the castle, and it was Ymbert de Bastarnay, whose influence at the royal court lasted through four reigns, who rebuilt the main château, with Renaissance dormers neatly framed by two castellated round towers. Shaded by huge cedar trees, the main portion of the castle still stands in the middle of the medieval fortifications, which now enclose a delightful garden. The different levels of the old walls have been used to make charming, rose-bowered sitting-out places, looking over the roofs of the old village.

Given the small scale of the place, there are a surprising number of fine Renaissance houses to be discovered lining its streets. Of particular note is the former chancellor's house, now the *mairie*. The old market-place, Les Halles des Cardeux, is a reminder of the wool trade that brought much of the village's prosperity, evident in the well-preserved main street.

Whether viewed from the ramparts of the medieval château (opposite) or across fields to the south (below), where the Renaissance church shares the honours with the château, the village fascinates in every corner.

The main street of
    Montrésor (left),
named after the nineteenth-
century Comte Branicki,
runs beneath the château
mound, which is itself
crossed by paths around the
original strongpoint
(opposite).

*T*he remains of the keep,
first built by Foulques
Nerra, and the ramparts
still survive (these pages).
The ruins of the latter
have been transformed
into inviting flower-
bedecked viewing
balconies and terraces.

Montrichard

LOIR-ET-CHER

One of the few strongholds of Foulques Nerra to remain pretty well intact looks down on the rooftops of this peaceful place on the banks of the Cher (these pages).

MONTRICHARD is always bustling with activity, especially on Saturday mornings, when the weekly market spreads itself through the narrow central streets and up into the market square. Its convenient position close to the Loire's most celebrated châteaux ensures that it is never short of visitors. The village boasts plenty of historical attractions of its own, however. The lofty *donjon* that rears over the village from its limestone cliff was built to guard an important cross-roads, where the ancient route between Blois and Poitiers met the Roman road from Tours to Bourges. An antique bridge carries the former over the Cher, its eight

arches, all at different heights, displaying a timeworn miscellany of architectural styles.

The *donjon* has lasted better than much of the rest of the fortress, but the view from the old ramparts is breathtaking, particularly when the castle's birds of prey are on display, swooping down from their vertiginously positioned perches, across the village roofs towards the river. Just below the keep is the village church of Sainte-Croix, built as the château's chapel and the setting for an ill-fated royal marriage in 1476. Louis XI had brought the fief of Montrichard under royal control when he took the throne in 1461. An inveterate schemer, he

A combination of Gothic and Renaissance decoration distinguishes the Hôtel d'Effiat (above) in the Rue Porte-au-Roi.

aimed to avert trouble in the future from the rebellious Dukes of Orléans by the expedient of marrying his own handicapped daughter Jeanne (aged twelve at the time) to the young Orléans heir, Louis. He calculated that the resultant sexless marriage would wipe out the Orléans succession altogether. His plans were eventually frustrated by the premature death of Charles VIII at Amboise. He left no heirs, so his crown passed to Louis d'Orléans, who remarried Anne of Brittany after he became Louis XII. Jeanne was free to retire to Bourges to found a religious order.

Scene of a popular Saturday market (above), Montrichard is truly dwarfed by Nerra's donjon and the remains of the curtain walls (opposite).

Richelieu

INDRE-ET-LOIRE

EVEN IN a region noted for extravagance and dotted with grandiose architectural fantasies, Richelieu stands apart. It is geographically apart, too, set in a remote corner of the Touraine, almost on the border with Poitou. Cardinal Richelieu, Louis XIII's chief minister, was the descendant of an impoverished aristocratic family from the area. At the height of his powers, he commissioned royal architects Jacques and Pierre Le Mercier to draw up plans for a monumental château, together with a fortified village, stylishly laid out according to his strict tastes. This was to be the capital of Richelieu's own principality, in which he enjoyed, among other demonstrations of his unassailable power, demolishing neighbouring châteaux that could rival his own.

   Although the château was demolished after the Revolution and its fabulous art collection dispersed, the village still stands grandly at the gates of the huge, empty *parc*. With its noble gateways and long straight streets, classical church and vast *halles,* it is a perfect seventeenth-century version of a classic French *bastide*. The Cardinal's tastes were indeed highly structured: the vehemently geometric plan of the village's rectangular layout is echoed exactly in the shape of each building plot. La Fontaine's description of Richelieu as 'the finest village in the universe', probably tells us more about the most prudent way to make fun of such a powerful individual than about the royal court's

The streets of the village (below) *were laid out with gates* (opposite) *to adjoin the park and château of Cardinal Richelieu* (left).

The houses on the Place des Réligieuses (left) *and the twin spires of the church of Notre-Dame* (opposite) *bespeak an architecturally grand ambition.*

true feelings about the project. Certainly Richelieu's ambition for his model village, that courtiers should buy up the *hôtels particuliers* and form a colony of learning and culture here, never came to much. It remains today, well-preserved and picturesque, a fascinating relic of the Cardinal's obsessions.

The village and the château together must have constituted an ensemble of quite extraordinary grandeur. As it is, the former is still an impressive piece of seventeenth-century planning. The simply named Grande Rue runs straight through the centre from the Porte de Chinon to the Porte de

Châtellerault towards the park of the château. It traverses two squares, the Place des Réligieuses and the Place du Marché, further emphasizing the symmetry of the Cardinal's grand design. Fittingly, a statue of the great man stands just before the park entrance at the end of the main street. The park itself still retains remnants of past glories. A pavilion now serves as a small museum of artefacts and documents relating to the Cardinal.

Saint-Aignan

LOIR-ET-CHER

DOMINATING the valley of the Cher from an eminence high above its southern bank, Saint-Aignan marks the meeting point of the three ancient provinces of Touraine, Sologne and Berry. The ancient citadel is spacious but steep-sided, leaving the village, with its narrow, twisting streets, to cluster tightly around its base. Above, two huge buildings rear against the skyline: the Renaissance wing of the château and, slightly below it, the collegiate church with its two towers.

The first wooden fort here was supplanted in the eleventh century by a stone fortress, whose main tower, the Tour Hagard, can still be seen. Predominantly, though, the château appears today to be what it had become by the sixteenth century – a grand lodging for a powerful local nobleman. This was Geoffrey de Donzy, whose family became successively counts in 1538, and dukes by 1663. Their rise in prosperity saw the reconstruction of the château in the most lavish of Renaissance styles. The impressive wing that looks out over the river is richly ornamented, particularly in its windows and octagonal, turreted staircase.

The village, with its collegiate church (above), lies beneath the château courtyard (right).

The château is still in private hands and has retained a seigneurial air. From the Hôtel de Ville in the square below, a tree-lined approach curves round the oldest part of the former fort, leading up to the entrance to an elegant park. Opposite, a *cour d'honneur* lies between the old and the new sections of the château, giving wonderful views over the Cher valley on the north side, and on the south, the slate and tile roofs of the village houses. From here a broad staircase curves grandly down to the collegiate church, graced with its fortified porch, and beneath, a Romanesque crypt with many surviving frescoes, including a *Christ in Majesty*.

*T*he view south from the château (opposite) *reveals a delightful picture of steep roofs and charming streets* (this page), *several of which run down to the river Cher.*

*M*ajestic steps (left) *lead down from the château to the collegiate church. Its crypt* (right *and* below), *used as a wine store after the Revolution, is decorated with a fresco of* The Crucifixion.

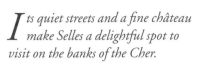

Selles-sur-Cher

LOIR-ET-CHER

THE PEACEFUL streets of Selles-sur-Cher, lined with prosperous-looking shops, offer no suggestion of the unusual and unpropitious beginnings of the settlement. The first name given to the settlement, Celles-Saint-Eusice, refers to the small number of monastic cells that were probably the first habitations to appear on the marshy and low-lying site. A young monk named Eusice, attached to the nearby abbey of Patriciacum, had set up a hermit's cell and oratory at this spot during the sixth century. He was joined by other monks, and they gained a formidable reputation in the locality for miraculous immunity from the regular flooding.

Another admirer of Eusice was the King Childebert, who met him as he came south to encounter the encroaching hordes of the Visigoths. Commanded by the king to predict the outcome of the coming battle, Eusice, following either divine guidance or common prudence, pronounced Childebert as victor. After the prediction came true, the returning monarch showed his appreciation by bestowing land for the foundation of a monastery, as well as donating a number of Visigoth prisoners-of-war (swiftly converted) to swell the numbers.

As the abbey grew in importance and size, and with it the surrounding settlement, its wealth was considered worth protecting from the regular invasions of land-hungry Normans from the north. The abbey itself was demolished after the Revolution, leaving only the fine church.

The château's Pavillon Doré (opposite) was added to a thirteenth-century fortress by Philippe de Béthune in the early seventeenth century. Among other outbuildings (this page), he also had a fine stable block built (left).

*F*amous for its château and gardens, Villandry nevertheless possesses corners of quiet charm within the village, especially around the parish church (above *and* opposite).

Villandry
INDRE-ET-LOIRE

LESS THAN twenty kilometres from the urban expanse of Tours, Villandry presents a restful and captivating ensemble: a noble château, gardens of an otherworldly perfection, and a tiny, peaceful village. The road that runs past along the Cher is not a busy one, and plans to construct a bridge across the river here, mooted in 1898, came to nothing.

A more significant date in Villandry's past is 1521, the year in which François I made Jean le Breton, Baron de Mondoucet, one of his Ministers of Finance. He was also to control the royal accounts at Blois and to be surveyor for his monarch's huge construction project at Chambord. When he bought the estate of Villandry (then called Colombiers) in 1532, le Breton demolished what was left of an ancient castle, and used its foundations to erect a Renaissance masterpiece of palatial proportions.

Experience gained at Chambord (which was to take many decades to complete) may have enabled le Breton to finish his château in record time: by January 1536 he was able to welcome his king, who paid an inaugural visit. On his death in 1542, le Breton's widow raised a stained-glass window to his memory, which can still be admired in the north apse of the parish church. The château stayed in the family until 1754, but following the Revolution it changed hands often; at one stage it was briefly owned by Napoleon.

Much honour is due to Dr. Joachim Carvallo, great-grandfather of the present owner, who bought Villandry in 1906. Not only did he rescue the château from demolition and bring it back to its Renaissance splendour: the ornamental gardens of that period had been swept away in that well-meaning but destructive frenzy of nineteenth-century fashion, when every landowner had to have a 'natural' park *à l'anglaise*. Happily, Dr. Carvallo was determined to recreate the gardens in their original style, and his enthusiasm and flair have been inherited by his great-grandson, with the help of a dedicated work-force.

This splendid walk-way runs beneath a vine-covered pergola (below), yet another of the many delights of Villandry.

The box garden (above), filled with symbols of love, is a tribute to the restorer's art. Beyond the potager (right) rises the château (opposite), built mainly in the sixteenth century by Jean le Breton, Secretary of State to François I.

Châteaux of the Loire

The terrace of the château at Amboise (above) provides magnificent views over the rooftops of the town to the river itself. Another river château is that of Ussé on the Indre (opposite), said to be the setting for Charles Perrault's Sleeping Beauty.

A TURBULENT HISTORY of invasions and quarrelling warlords, succeeded by the fabulous wealth of the royal courts, has made the Loire region a living history of the château. The first simple wooden palisades were often constructed on top of the nearest hill, providing the local populace with a defensive centre from which to watch for the approaching invader. Sometimes a central watch-tower was built inside the palisade; this in turn evolved into the square keep or *donjon*.

The early *donjons* were ruggedly functional, more garrison than dwelling, although building in stone allowed for a more massive and compact design, requiring fewer defenders and allowing less cramped accommodation. A fine example of this is the wonderfully restored, four-storeyed *donjon* that looms over the Loire at Oudon. The trend towards a less spartan existence was continued after the first crusaders returned from the Near East, where they

had been astonished by the level of opulence in the sultans' palaces. They had also learnt important lessons in the increasingly sophisticated science of fortification. Moats were dug deeper, double ramparts and geometrically correct angles of fire could be incorporated into new designs which could now be built in open country.

By the sixteenth century, however, with returning armies under the spell of the Italian Renaissance, comfort and decoration were more important than impregnability; it now became fashionable to demonstrate power and status by ostentatious building rather than by prowess of arms. François I led the way with the impracticably colossal Chambord, followed by the exquisite creations of his courtiers at Azay-le-Rideau and Villandry. The *tuffeau* from which many of these confections were crafted is said to become with age more durable, whiter and more beautiful!

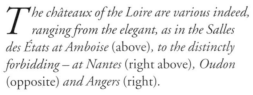

The châteaux of the Loire are various indeed, ranging from the elegant, as in the Salles des États at Amboise (above), *to the distinctly forbidding – at Nantes* (right above), *Oudon* (opposite) *and Angers* (right).

The grandeur of the château at Chaumont-sur-Loire (this page) bespeaks its royal connections as one of the residences of Catherine de' Medici: the main apartments (left); the main staircase (below left); and the keep from the east (below).

The buildings of Valençay (opposite) date from the mid sixteenth century; massive though they are, they were clearly meant to impress by their decorative appearance rather than by their defensive utility.

*O*ne of the prettiest of all the Loire châteaux is
Chenonceau (this page). *Its main pavilions
stretch across the river Cher (above)* beyond the
garden of Catherine de' Medici. *Another garden
with significant historical associations is that of
Diane de Poitiers (right),* the mistress of Henri II.

A centre of the Renaissance in France, Blois (this page) was especially loved by Louis XII and, later, François I. One of the legacies of the latter is the magnificent octagonal staircase, seen here in the foreground (far left *and* below). *A copy of an original statue of Louis XII graces the alcove above the Flamboyant gateway of the façade* (left).

Around Angers and Nantes

ON THE SOUTHERN BANK of the Loire, Touraine gives way gracefully to its western neighbour, Anjou. The two villages of Candes-Saint-Martin and Montsoreau lie close to each other. Yet they lie in different *départements* and, for a thousand years before that, in two often opposed kingdoms. By this stage, the limestone cliffs that downstream from Orléans were on the north bank, have switched to the south. Opposite lies the giant flat plain of the Varenne de Bourgueil, alluvial silt deposited by the river and kept from flooding by Henri II's embankment.

After Angers, the wine-growing activity intensifies again: the steep, stony slopes of the vineyards at Savennières and at the famous Château de Serrant produce a very different white wine from that of the Coteaux du Layon, directly to the south, and from that of the huge Muscadet *appellations* west of Ancenis.

By this point the Loire is broad and deep enough in its natural state to allow the more enterprising visitor to sample the delights of river travel, perhaps on a traditional flat-bottomed *gabare*. And not many kilometres downstream there is no doubt of the river's navigability. Nantes is still massively involved in the importation of goods by sea, although the shipbuilding yards opposite Trentemoult have largely fallen silent. In contrast to the noisy manoeuvres of the huge freighters that patronize France's third largest port, wonderfully peaceful countryside can be found close by, along the wooded valley of the Erdre to the north or the vineyards by the Sèvre to the south.

The château at Saumur looks out over the river Loire and the Pont Cessart.

Baugé
MAINE-ET-LOIRE

THE UBIQUITOUS Count of Anjou, Foulques Nerra, built the first defensive citadel at Baugé in 1000, where the present Place de l'Europe can be found. It was to be a descendant of his, a Plantagenet, crowned king of England, who would one day be the cause of its destruction. After his crushing defeat of the French at Agincourt, Henry V was poised to overrun a country, the power of whose royal family was almost spent. France still had some allies left, however, and an army of Scots who landed at La Rochelle in 1419 was to win a major victory over the English forces at Baugé two years later.

Under the command of the Duke of Clarence, younger brother of the English king, 2,500

E legant nineteenth-century ironwork embellishes a balcony in the Rue de l'Église (above) *and the village bandstand on the Place de l'Europe* (right).

Q uiet days in Baugé – the streets of the village yield many peaceful corners: from the Rue de l'Église (above); the Ruelle Bois-Hube (right above and opposite above); the fullers' mill on the Rue Altrée (right below).

mounted troops and archers tried to attack the town, which was garrisoned by a Franco-Scottish force. As the bridge at Baugé over the river Couasnon was too strongly defended, an attempt was made to ford it down the hill at what is now Vieil-Baugé. Those who survived the crossing were cut off as they attempted to climb the narrow lane by La-Roche-Perron. Ferocious fighting left the English commander and 1000 of his men dead, with 500 taken prisoner.

This triumph did not secure the future of the fortress at Baugé: fourteen years later Duchess

Yolanda of Aragon was forced to burn the citadel to the ground to prevent the English from occupying it. Her son, Duke Réné of Anjou, had nothing to inherit but a ruin. Undaunted, he built a new château just to the north, inside the defensive walls. Under the *ancien régime*, five royal jurisdictions were set up, and the numerous royal counsellors who ruled over these administrations housed themselves in no less than forty-six grand stone-built town-houses, giving the streets of Baugé their imposing appearance. Up the sloping Rue de l'Église, the eleventh-century church of Saint-Laurent was replaced by a chapel dedicated to St. Peter in 1593.

The grandest architecture of Baugé is grouped close to the Place de l'Europe; the church, the château, and the Tribunal.

Beaufort-en-Vallée

MAINE-ET-LOIRE

A STATUE of Jeanne de Laval stands in the middle of the main square of Beaufort-en-Vallée. The village has every reason to pay grateful tribute to her memory. Her husband, Duke Réné of Anjou, acquired the remains of a castle that stood on a commanding knoll overlooking the Loire valley to the south. In addition to the huge building work he was then undertaking in the castle and the town at Angers, he also oversaw the remodelling of the castle at Beaufort, and local lore has it that Jeanne was extensively involved in its planning and execution. This was certainly her principal residence and the octagonal tower from this period is named after her. Royal patronage (Réné is often referred to as the 'good king', although he was actually only claimant to the Kingdom of Sicily) was certainly good for Beaufort, and by the following century a lively trading community had sprung up around the fortifications.

Peace and prosperity meant less need for a fortress in full working order, and by 1635 a royal edict from Louis XIII authorized the inhabitants to help themselves to building materials from the castle as it fell into ruin.

The village itself, however, became much grander, mainly because of the cultivation of hemp in the area. A royal manufactory of sailcloth was set up in 1750; its success saw the population rise to a high of 6,000. The fine stone houses and, later, the wonderfully pretentious *mairie* attest to this prosperity. The palatial Halles dates from 1842.

*B*eaufort's original prosperity was assured in the fifteenth century by the patronage of Duke René of Anjou. A statue of his wife, Jeanne de Laval, stands in the main square (opposite). Later economic success came from sail-making, prompting the building of the palatial Halles (above) in 1842.

The remains of the castle (opposite) stand on a knoll above the village, giving a fine view of the church of Notre-Dame (below). Also below the castle mound is the École du Château (right).

Chenillé-Changé
MAINE-ET-LOIRE

AN ENTRY in the local archive, dated 1551, records that 'a nobleman, esquire and seigneur of the Rues Chenillé and de Lorrière, sold to the Demoiselle Jehanne de la Daugère, lady of Varennes, the mill of Chaussé de Chenillé, sited on the river Maine, beside the village called Chenillé'. In fact, the tradition of water-mills on this spot stretches back for a thousand years. The Mayenne river arrives at Chenillé having negotiated a particularly rocky and narrow stretch, giving the water-flow enough concentrated force to power two mills, which face each other across a thundering weir.

The mill on the village side is still in operation: four floors of clanking machinery, powered by a massive seven-metre water-wheel, which can be inspected from a safe distance. The battlements are a testament not to a warlike past but to late nineteenth-century whimsy, when the mill was rebuilt after a fire.

This out-of-the-way river hamlet on the Maine is remarkable for the quality of its architecture and its generally immaculate appearance (these pages).

As well as being an elegant boating centre for the river Maine, the village is also a popular spot for anglers (above). *This fox-terrier, on good terms with all the village householders, keeps a watchful eye on the mill* (opposite).

Another recent historical event, the Franco-Prussian war of the 1870s, was responsible for one of Chenillé-Changé's very distinctive features – a figure of the Virgin of the Sacred Heart, which stands on top of a hill to the north of the village. The owners of the Château des Rues, to the south of the village, vowed to raise an ex-voto if their lands were spared the ravages of war. Anjou was at the time panicked by the approach of the Prussian army, which had advanced as far as Le Mans. The promise was kept three years later, and there is a splendid view of the village, its mill and the river from the statue's base.

The little church at the centre of the village is a good example of a simple Romanesque construction that has not suffered at the hands of 'improvers'. The walls of the nave were raised in the eleventh century, and a hundred years later it was lengthened with the addition of a choir, which terminates in a simple, semicircular apse. Later, in the years just before the Revolution, the original bell-tower, whose bells were hung in an open embrasure, was replaced by the present bell-tower, topped by an elegant spire. Treasures inside include a rustic statue of St. James, dug up in the parish priest's garden where it had doubtless been buried to escape the iconoclastic attentions of the post-Revolutionary mobs.

The original fifteenth-century keep (left) contrasts peculiarly with the overall Italianate style of the village (opposite), the result of rebuilding after destruction by fire during the Vendée uprising.

Clisson

LOIRE-ATLANTIQUE

THE VISITOR looking down on Clisson, nestling contentedly in the valley of the Sèvre, would find it hard to imagine that just over two hundred years ago almost all that would have been seen of the village were smouldering ruins. During the bitter reprisals after the Vendée uprising, Republican *colonnes d'enfer* slaughtered hundreds of local people and left almost no buildings standing, an exception being the fifteenth-century Halles, which were used to garrison their troops.

Clisson's fortunes turned when the active imagination of a visiting painter from Nantes saw in the shattered village the potential for realizing an aesthetic dream. Together with his friend, sculptor Frédéric Lemot, then returning with a passion for all things Italian from studies in Rome, Pierre Cacault set about the reconstruction of the village. The grounds of Lemot's own villa, La Garenne Lemot, are filled with features which evoke the Roman *campagna*: umbrella pines, grottoes,

*T*he streets of the village look almost as though they have been removed from some Tuscan town (this page). *Equally Italianate, though more Roman in inspiration, is the Villa La Garenne, built by Frédéric Lemot for his own use (opposite).*

belvederes and temples. The villa's spacious terrace, high above the river, looks out on the rebuilt village and over to the Temple of Friendship, designed as a romantic resting-place for Lemot's own remains. Many of the public and private buildings added since have been built in an Italianate style, including mills and tanneries along the banks of the Sèvre. In place of the destroyed Église Collégiale stands a miniature version of the church of SS. Peter and Paul in Rome. The whole effect, on a Sunday afternoon when the streets are full of local families out for their post-prandial stroll, is of a model village, inadvertently built to full scale. The ruined bulk of the fifteenth-century castle contrasts strangely with a scene of Mediterranean gaiety.

The park of La Garenne-Lemot (left) is full of Italianate features, including the tower-house for the gardener. The castle keep (above) was the scene of a terrible massacre of the inhabitants of the village by Revolutionary militiamen.

The Abbess's lodging (right) is one of the many elegant buildings of the whole complex. Each of the eight semi-circular alcoves of the extraordinary Romanesque kitchens (opposite) used to contain an oven; the fanciful roof with lozenge-shaped tiles was added during restoration in the early twentieth century.

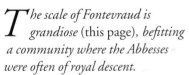

The scale of Fontevraud is grandiose (this page), befitting a community where the Abbesses were often of royal descent.

can be found a memorial chapel dedicated to St. Catherine of Alexandria. Its distinctive *lanterne des morts* used to illuminate the village cemetery before this was moved inside the abbey walls. Finally, on the outskirts of the village, the chapel of Notre-Dame-de-la-Pitié recalls a period when the plague threatened village and abbey alike. Members of the order who took refuge in the woods to survive erected this little chapel in thanks to a merciful Divinity.

At the centre of the whole complex is the abbey church and the Sainte-Marie cloister (below and far right). There is some especially fine carving in the chapter-house (right).

La Meilleraie
LOIRE-ATLANTIQUE

LIKE TRENTEMOULT, its counterpart downstream at Nantes, La Meilleraie is a settlement whose close proximity to the banks of the Loire announces a very practical reason for its being there. The fifty or so fishermen's cottages that line its two streets could not be more convenient for the job in hand, but they are also perilously vulnerable to flooding. Almost every front garden sports some variety of flat-bottomed boat as a precaution against a sudden rise in the level of the river.

The fishermen of La Meilleraie traditionally had a reputation for lawlessness: '*refuge de brigands, sous l'ancien comme sous le nouveau régime*', as one Republican administrator put it. They were certainly successful in subverting efforts by the Dukes of Ancenis to enclose and fortify the village, and came up in court regularly for refusing to be pressed into the King's Militia. The new *régime* that arrived after the Revolution was no more popular, with a huge new Republican army to be recruited, and new taxes and duties to be levied on their fishing livelihoods. Soon most of the men of the village were helping the loyalist insurgents sack Republican headquarters in neighbouring Varades, and were also involved in supplying the attempted blockade of Ancenis. In the retributions that

Lying close to the level of the river Loire, this modest fishermen's settlement is overlooked by the grander village of Saint-Florent-le-Vieil.

followed, after Republicans regained control of the northern banks of the Loire, more than half the village's houses were burnt to the ground.

Although the little cobbled slipway that forms the 'port' is still surrounded by river-craft, the once rich harvest of eels, shad, lamprey and pike from the Loire has dwindled. Boats still put out from here to make their way to one of the two large trawling barges moored below the bridge, but falling fish stocks have further limited their strictly seasonal operations. When they are working, in continuous day-and-night shifts, spectators on the bridge can enjoy a magnificent view of the bringing-in of the catch.

The monastic church of Saint-Florent (opposite) *looks grandly across the river to the more modest buildings of La Meilleraie on the other bank* (left *and* above).

Le Lion-d'Angers

MAINE-ET-LOIRE

JULIUS CAESAR'S legions are thought to have established a garrison town here during the campaign against the Gauls. Traces of a Roman road and a crossing of the river Oudon dating from the same period have been discovered, and it is generally accepted that the village's name comes from a corruption of 'legion'. The first church was built at Le Lion-d'Angers around the year 1000. The local saint to whom it was dedicated, St. Martin, was a monk who founded the notable abbey of Vertou near Nantes. It was he who led the evangelizing efforts in the region, from the end of the sixth century.

The *quais* on the river Mayenne, which once saw busy traffic between the important towns of Laval and Angers, looks on to another, quite different claim to fame for the locality. Behind a screen of poplars, there is a spacious racecourse that forms the larger part of the equestrian Isle-Briand. This land belonged for several centuries to the de Tredern family, who in later years remodelled and enlarged their château in Louis-Quinze style, and followed the fashion of the times in setting out a model farm. In 1972 this became the site of the Haras National (the national stud), which from 1797 had been squeezed into a tiny site in Angers.

The houses on the Quai d'Anjou were the witnesses of busy river traffic along the river Mayenne for centuries.

The massive medieval fortifications (opposite) around the much remodelled Château de Bellay look out over the village rooftops and the Place du Château (right).

Montreuil-Bellay
MAINE-ET-LOIRE

IT WAS FOULQUES NERRA, Count of Anjou in the eleventh century, who recognized the potential of this hilltop site, and established a stronghold to protect his domain from neighbouring Poitou. He gave command of the resulting fortress to his vassal Berlay. Successive generations of the Berlay (later Bellay) family became less loyal to their Anjou overlords. As they juggled their support between the Count and the sovereign of France, numerous sieges tested the increasingly sophisticated defences of the château. At length their fate was sealed by a poorly timed re-alliance with Anjou, now under the control of the Plantagenets, which coincided with that family's succession to the English throne. So it was the French Philippe-Auguste who finally overran the château and burnt it to the ground.

The Harcourt family were either luckier than the Bellays, or lived in less fraught times. It was they who, during the fifteenth century, built the majority of the present-day buildings inside the former

Though dominated by the château and its ramparts (opposite), Montreuil-Bellay still manages to create an air of intimacy in corners like these (this page).

The foot-bridge to the château (opposite) was added in the nineteenth century to give access to the chapel which also served as the village church. Softening the military aspect of the medieval château (right), the Renaissance pavilion (below) looks out over formal gardens.

defences. The ancient gatehouse and bastion were remodelled, and inside the safety of the enclosure, a graceful Renaissance wing was added, with a lordly staircase. What is now the collegiate church was also built inside the walls, first serving as the family's private chapel. Only when the much smaller village church of Saint-Pierre, by the river Thouet, collapsed in the early nineteenth century, did this become the villagers' church, and a much less agressively war-like bridge and entrance-gate were built to allow access from the village.

There used to be numerous fortified villages in Anjou; Montreuil-Bellay alone survives with more than half its fifteenth-century walls intact, and four of its eight defensive gates. The chief among these, the massive Porte Saint-Jean, still looms over the southern approaches towards Thouars. Its two hefty bastions are studded with large round cobbles, adding greatly to its air of menacing defiance and strength.

Oudon
LOIRE-ATLANTIQUE

THE FORTRESS TOWER of Oudon altogether dominates the village in which it stands, and commands the broad expanse of the Loire as it sweeps downstream from Ancenis towards Nantes. The river here marks the boundary between the ancient kingdoms of Brittany and Anjou, and it was certainly in the interests of Brittany to secure allies to guard this border. Two hundred years before the present tower was built, a former château was overrun by besieging forces, four times in succession. Small wonder that only a small section of the curtain wall survived to be incorporated in the major rebuilding which started in 1392.

It was Alain de Malestroit, scion of a family of proven loyalty to the Duchy of Brittany, who was given permission to refortify the site. It is to him that we owe the superb octagonal keep, on four floors with a magnificent fireplace on each level.

The monumental example in the top storey is the most ornate, a showy affair that suggests that the tower was designed for gracious living, as well as for the grimmer business of warfare. A recent restoration project means that visitors can now reach the top of the tower and enjoy the splendid views. The de Malestroit family also had to keep an eye on the rival clan of the Penthierre-Rohan, of less dependable loyalty to Brittany. Their castle, at

Towers of secular and ecclesiastical power respectively dominate the village: the restored donjon *to the left, and the spire of Saint-Martin to the right.*

O udon's original prosperity,
evidenced in the many fine
public and private buildings, was
founded on the traffic along the Loire.

Champtoceaux on the opposite bank of the Loire,
was duly destroyed in a raid by Jean V, Duke of
Brittany. The rivalry could well have been about
more than political allegiances: Oudon had a busy
port where the river Havre, navigable in those days
as far as Couffé, flows into the Loire, whereas
Champtoceaux had the right to levy duties on river
traffic coming down from Ancenis. Part of the
thirteenth-century toll station still survives, jutting
out into the navigation channel.

At the confluence of the Sèvre and Maine lie some of the best vineyards of the whole Loire valley, mainly planted with the Muscadet grape, sometimes known as the Melon de Bourgogne (these pages).

At the Château du Coing (left *and* opposite) *the wine is made* sur lie, *maturing on its sediment for six months. This traditional wine press (below) was taken from the cellars of the Domaine de la Cantrie, destroyed after the Revolution.*

Savennières

MAINE-ET-LOIRE

THE VILLAGE of Savennières, hiding its celebrated vines behind high stone walls, gives its *appellation* to some of the region's finest wines. Produced in small quantities from the Chenin Blanc grape, the wines are powerful and long-lived, and include the well-known *grands crus* of La Roche-aux-Moines, and the nearby Coulée de Serrant, along the Loire towards Angers.

This area, on the north bank of the river, was settled by the Romans for most of the 400 years of their rule. Whether or not they availed themselves of the perfect conditions for producing wine is a matter of conjecture, but it was certainly the quality of its wines that assured Savennières an important position in the twelfth century, when Anjou started to settle to peace and prosperity under Plantagenet rule. By this time it was under

The spire of the Romanesque church rises above the vineyards and the potager *of the Domaine du Closel* (below *and* opposite).

the protection of the powerful Abbaye de Saint-Serge in Angers, and not long after Henry II acceded to the English throne, the notable parish church, dedicated to St. Peter, was greatly enlarged and extended. This remarkable survival of the primitive Romanesque is said to be one of the oldest churches in Anjou, if not in France. Certainly, the façades to the south and west, adjoining the two doors to the church, display a very ancient-looking mixture of materials: black pebbles and rows of bricks aligned diagonally in a herring-bone pattern. This oldest surviving part of the church could well date back to Carolingian times. The south door, installed with other improvements in the twelfth century, contrasts pleasantly with its surround: twin arches and, above, a cornice held up by a row of ten sculpted medallions of grotesque heads.

Around the church, high-walled streets lead between some stately stone houses, a fine *mairie* and a shady village green. At the top of the village there is a grassy lane, the Chemin des Perrières, by means of which the famous vineyards can be explored. These include the hill-top Clos de Papillon, which gives a magnificent view of the village and the great river beyond. These vines lie in the Domaine du Closel, whose fine eighteenth-century mansion, surrounded by cedars, sits below its vineyards, facing south towards the Loire. Here wine has been the family business for many generations, under the management of the redoubtable de Jessey family, whose considerable expertise is by tradition passed down the female line.

Although the spire of Saint-Pierre (opposite) dates only from the nineteenth century, other parts of the church, like the south wall (above), are thought to be among the oldest ecclesiastical building in France.

The main house of the Domaine du Closel (left and opposite) has seen several generations of the same family (de Jessey) produce the famous wine of the village.

Sucé-sur-Erdre
LOIRE-ATLANTIQUE

*T*he tower of Saint-Étienne
(left) *looks over a village
now known as a centre for
pleasure boating* (above).

TODAY'S VISITORS to Sucé may well catch their first
glimpse of this pretty village from aboard one of the
excursion boats that make the trip from Nantes,
fifteen kilometres to the south. The Erdre is a
delightful river to explore; as it winds gently
through the countryside, the wooded banks
disclose a number of delectable châteaux and
demeures de plaisance. Sucé itself is a modest
crossing-point of the little river, which until the
sixteenth-century was only a tiny rivulet watering
the rich pasturage and buckwheat fields of the area.
Then a dam was built at the Nantes end to make
navigation possible.

　　Among the fine houses dotted about the parish
(in one of which the philosopher René Descartes

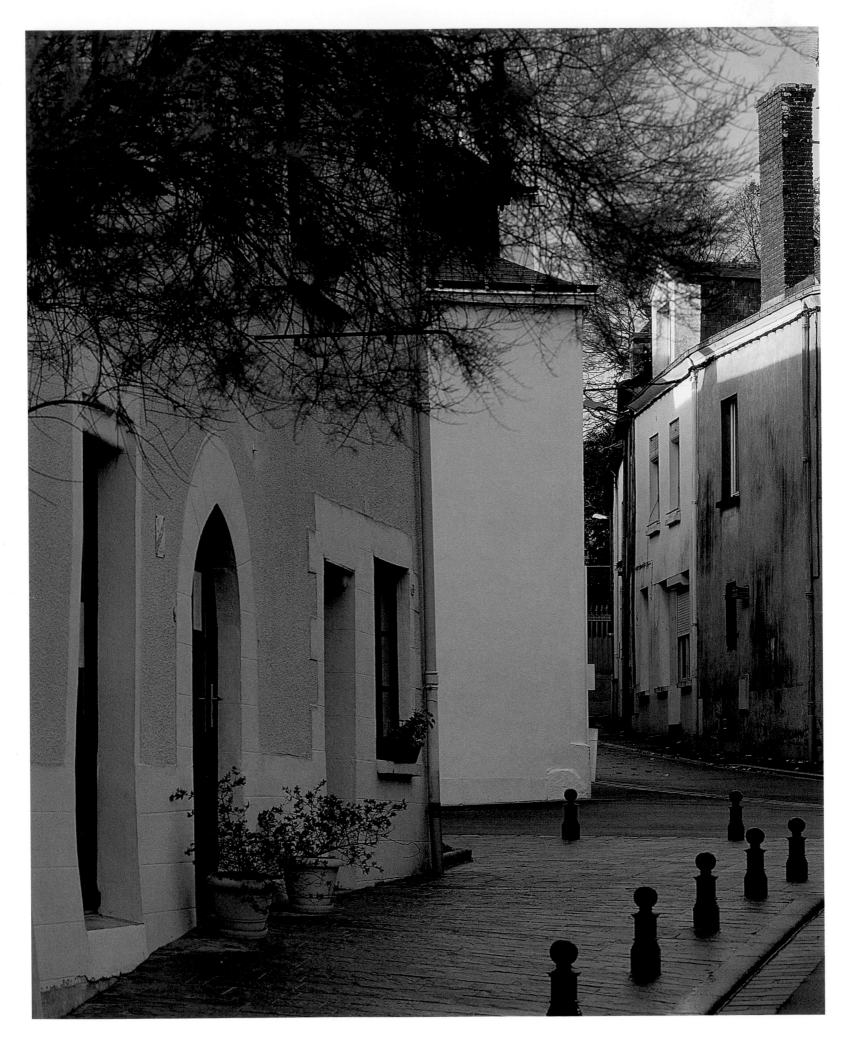

Q uiet streets of sixteenth-century houses welcome the visitor to Sucé-sur-Erdre (these pages).

spent part of his childhood) is that of La Cour Gaillard, where a number of Huguenots were able to settle after the 1598 Edict of Nantes granted them freedom to worship. Indeed, they built a temple there, installed a priest, and barges laden with adherents singing psalms used to row upstream every Sunday, according to one local historian. The Protestants were forced to decamp after the Edict was revoked in 1685, and the temple

was pulled down. There is still a Rue des Protestants in the village to testify to their presence there.

Above Sucé, the Erdre (whose name was only joined to that of the village as recently as 1973) joins with the sizeable Lac de Mazerolles, a magnet for fishermen and wildfowlers, as well as for the colourful sailing boats that are berthed beside the village's grassy riverbanks.

*T*rentemoult's streets, shops and hidden corners *(these pages) are an unpretentious reflection of the simple existence of the original fisherfolk.*

*T*he journey along the Loire is over: at Paimbœuf (Loire-Atlantique) on the south shore, looking eastwards.

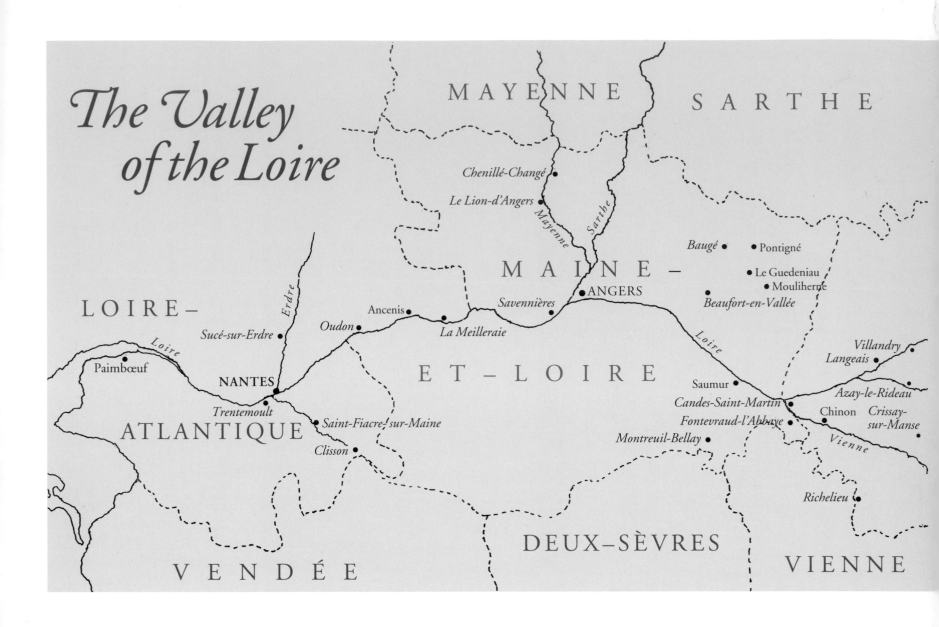

The Valley of the Loire

MAYENNE

SARTHE

Chenillé-Changé

Le Lion-d'Angers

Baugé   • Pontigné

MAINE-

• Le Guedeniau

• Mouliherne

Savennières   •Angers

Beaufort-en-Vallée

LOIRE-

Ancenis

Villandry

Sucé-sur-Erdre   Oudon

Langeais

La Meilleraie

Paimbœuf

ET–LOIRE

Saumur

Azay-le-Rideau

NANTES

Candes-Saint-Martin

Chinon   Crissay-sur-Manse

Trentemoult

Fontevraud-l'Abbaye

ATLANTIQUE

Saint-Fiacre-sur-Maine

Montreuil-Bellay •

Clisson

Richelieu

DEUX–SÈVRES

VENDÉE

VIENNE

Eating in the Loire

FRESH LOCAL PRODUCE in great variety, and a strong regional tradition of cooking: such are the archetypal attractions of a visit to France. The Loire valley, long known as the garden of France, is richly productive, and its *cuisine*, unfussy and straightforward, reflects the range of its terrain.

The river itself still provides a good range of freshwater fish: the *sandre* (pike-perch), famously served with *beurre blanc* (melted butter sauce flavoured with shallots), stewed eels (*anguilles*) and the simple and delicious *friture* (a fried assortment of whitebait-sized river fish). *Rillons* and *rillettes*, charcuterie originating from around Tours, are popular starters, served with toast and enjoyed with a white wine from Vouvray or Montlouis. The historic forests of Berry and the Sologne, haunts of the hunting-obsessed royal courts of the past, continue to harbour plenty of game. Pheasant, carefully braised in a wine and brandy sauce, or roast wild boar, are often

198

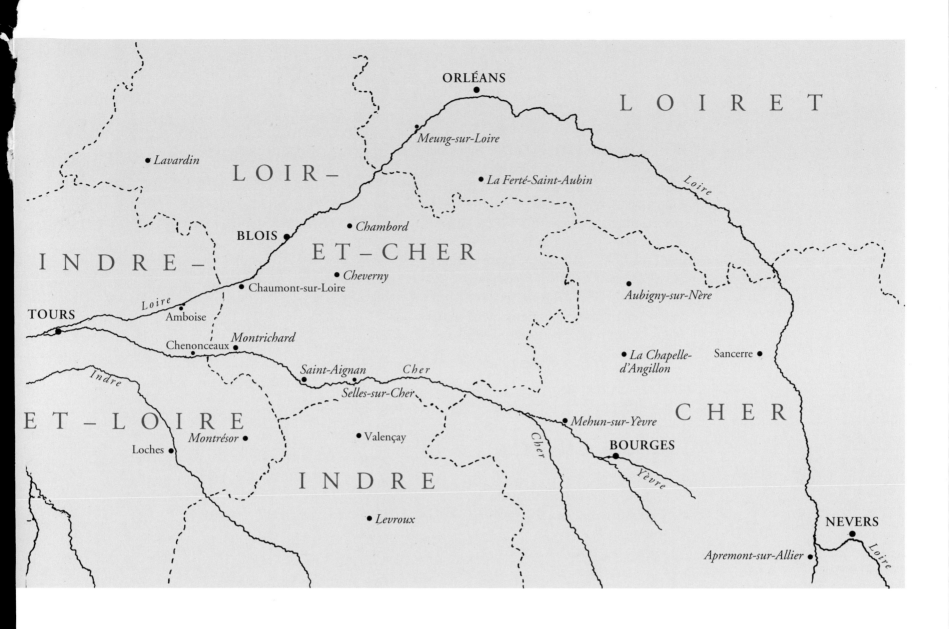

washed down with a red wine from Chinon and Bourgeuil. These *appellations* are gaining in popularity outside France, having long been overlooked in favour of their southern competitors – but on their home territory they are particularly delicious, light and almost flowery in character, but rich in fruit. The famous white wines from Sancerre and Pouilly go admirably with the goat cheeses of the Loire: the *crottin de Chavignol* from a wine-making village near Sancerre, and the softer, charcoal-encrusted variety from Selles-sur-Cher.

The orchards of the Loire are as abundant as its vineyards, and most local desserts feature some of the many fruits grown here. The Sologne was the birthplace of that inspired culinary invention, responsible for saving the sanity and reputation of many a hard-pressed dinner-party host, the famous *tarte tatin,* or upside-down apple tart.

A Travellers' Guide

While every effort has been made to ensure that the information given in the following entries is correct, the author and the publisher cannot be held responsible for any inadvertent inaccuracies. Opening dates and times of local attractions change seasonally and sometimes alter from year to year; it is always advisable to check with the venue or the nearest tourist information office in advance. The restaurants and hotels listed are the personal choice of the author and photographer; intending visitors should consult local listings and the *Michelin Guide to France*.

AROUND ORLÉANS

Apremont-sur-Allier, Cher

SIGHTS & EVENTS
Château and *Parc Floral*, open April to September; tel. (0248) 775500.
INFORMATION
Mairie; tel. (0248) 584020.

Aubigny-sur-Nère, Cher

WHERE TO STAY
Hôtel La Fontaine, 2 avenue Général Leclerc; tel. (0248) 580259.
Hôtel-Restaurant La Solognote, 18 km north-west; tel. (0248) 585029.
WHERE TO EAT
Hôtel-Restaurant La Solognote (see above).
Restaurant La Chaumière (also has rooms), 2 rue Paul Lasnier; tel. (0248) 580401.
Restaurant Bien Aller, 3 rue des Dames; tel. (0248) 580392.
Château de la Verrerie (also has rooms), 10 km south-east; tel.(0248)815160.
INFORMATION
1 rue de l'Église; tel. (0248)584020.

La Chapelle-d'Angillon, Cher

SIGHTS & EVENTS
Château, open all year; guided tours; tel. (0248) 734110.
WHERE TO STAY
See under **Aubigny-sur-Nère**.

WHERE TO EAT
See under **Aubigny-sur-Nère**.
INFORMATION
Mairie; tel. (0248) 734341.

La Ferté-Saint-Aubin, Loiret

SIGHTS & EVENTS
Château, guided tours daily, kitchen demonstrations; tel. (0238) 765272.
WHERE TO STAY
Hôtel L'Orée des Chênes, 3 km north-east; tel. (0238) 648400.
Mme. Beau at *La Ferme des Foucaults* (guest house), 9 km east; tel. (0238) 769441.
WHERE TO EAT
Restaurant La Ferme de la Lande, 4 km north-east; tel. (0238) 766437.
Auberge de l'Écu de France, 6 rue Général Leclerc; tel. (0238) 646922.
Restaurant La Sauvagine, 53 rue Général Leclerc; tel. (0238) 766223.
INFORMATION
Rue des Jardins; tel. (0238) 646793.

Mehun-sur-Yèvre, Cher

WHERE TO STAY
Hôtel-Restaurant La Croix Blanche, 164 rue Jeanne d'Arc; tel. (0248) 573001.
Hôtel-Restaurant Le Lion d'Or, 18 place 14 juillet; tel. (0248) 573060.
WHERE TO EAT
Restaurant Les Abiès, 89 avenue Jean Châtelet; tel. (0248) 573931.
Restaurant La Ribotte, Le Paradis; tel. (0248) 571658.
INFORMATION
Place 14 juillet; tel. (0248) 573551.

Meung-sur-Loire, Loiret

SIGHTS & EVENTS
Château, open daily; tel. (0238) 443647.
WHERE TO EAT
Café du Commerce; tel. (0238) 443235.
Auberge Saint-Jacques, 60 rue Général de Gaulle; tel. (0238) 443039.
INFORMATION
42 rue Jehan de Meung; tel. (0238) 443228.

Orléans, Loiret

WHERE TO STAY
Sanotel, 16 quai Saint-Laurent;
tel. (0238) 544765.
WHERE TO EAT
Restaurant Chancellerie, place Martroi;
tel. (0238) 535754.
INFORMATION
Place Albert 1ère; tel. (0238) 240505.

AROUND BLOIS
AND TOURS

Amboise, Indre-et-Loire

SIGHTS & EVENTS
Château, open all year;
tel. (0247) 570098.
WHERE TO STAY
Hotel-Restaurant Château de Pray,
3 km east, at Chargé; tel. (0247) 572367.
WHERE TO EAT
Restaurant Manoir Saint-Thomas,
1 mail Saint-Thomas; tel.(0247) 572252.
INFORMATION
Quai Général de Gaulle;
tel. (0247) 470928.

Azay-le-Rideau, Indre-et-Loire

SIGHTS & EVENTS
Château, open all year;
tel. (0247) 454204.
WHERE TO STAY
Hôtel-Restaurant Grand Monarque,
place République; tel. (0247) 454008.
Hôtel Le Biencourt, rue Balzac;
tel. (0247) 452075.
Mme. de Drezigue, *Le Clos Philippa*
(guest house); tel. (0247) 452649.
WHERE TO EAT
Restaurant L'Aigle d'Or, 10 avenue A. Riche;
tel. (0247) 452458.
Restaurant Les Grottes, rue Pineau;
tel. (0247) 452104.
INFORMATION
5 place de l'Europe;
tel. (0247) 454440.

Blois, Loir-et-Cher

SIGHTS & EVENTS
Château, open all year; tel. (0254) 780662.
WHERE TO STAY
Anne de Bretagne, 31 avenue Jean-Laigret;
tel. (0254) 780538.
WHERE TO EAT
L'Orangerie du Château,
1 avenue Jean-Laigret; tel. (0254) 780536.
INFORMATION
3 avenue Jean-Laigret; tel. (0254) 904141.

Candes-Saint-Martin, Indre-et-Loire

WHERE TO STAY
M. Nourri (guest house), 3 km north-west,
at Turquant; tel. (0241) 381611.
La Fontaine (guest house), 46 route de
Compostelle; tel. (0247) 958366.
WHERE TO EAT
L'Auberge de la Route d'Or, 2 place de
l'Église; tel. (0247) 958110.
Restaurant Diane de Meridor, 0.5 km north-
west, at Montsoreau; tel. (0241) 517176.

Chambord, Loir-et-Cher

SIGHTS & EVENTS
Château, open all year; tel. (0254) 504000.
Horse displays, May to September;
tel. (0254) 203101.
WHERE TO STAY
Hôtel-Restaurant Grand Saint-Michel,
103 place Saint-Michel; tel. (0254) 203131.
WHERE TO EAT
Restaurant Le Chambourdin, route de
Bracieux; tel. (0254) 203264.
Restaurant La Crêperie Solognote;
tel. (0254) 203675.
INFORMATION
At the château; tel. (0254) 203486.

Chenonceaux, Indre-et-Loire

SIGHTS & EVENTS
Château, open all year; tel. (0247) 239007.
WHERE TO STAY
*Hôtel-Restaurant Hostellerie du Château de
l'Isle*, at Civray; tel. (0247) 238009.

WHERE TO EAT
See above.
INFORMATION
1 rue du Dr. Bretonneau;tel. (0247) 239445.

Cheverny, Loir-et-Cher

SIGHTS & EVENTS
Château, open daily; tel. (0254) 799629.
WHERE TO STAY
Hôtel-Restaurant Trois Marchands;
tel. (0254) 799644.
Hôtel-Restaurant Saint-Hubert;
tel. (0254) 799660.
Hôtel Château de Breuil, 3 km west;
tel. (0254) 442020.
WHERE TO EAT
Restaurant Pousse Rapière;
tel. (0254) 799423.
INFORMATION
4 avenue de Cheverny; tel. (0254) 799563.

Crissay-sur-Manse, Indre-et-Loire

SIGHTS & EVENTS
Honey production, M. Laubigeau;
tel. (0247) 952281.
WHERE TO STAY
L'Auberge; tel. (0247) 585811.
WHERE TO EAT
See above.
INFORMATION
Mairie; tel. (0247) 585405.

Langeais, Indre-et-Loire

SIGHTS & EVENTS
Château, open all year; tel. (0247) 967260.
Market, Sunday mornings.
WHERE TO STAY
Hôtel-Restaurant Errard Hosten,
2 rue Gambetta; tel. (0247) 968212.
Hôtel-Restaurant Château de Rochecotte,
10 km west; tel. (0247) 961616.
Mme. Venot Marion, 28 rue Foulques
Nerra (guest house); tel. (0247) 966845.
WHERE TO EAT
See first two entries above.
INFORMATION
Place 14 juillet; tel. (0247) 965822.

Lavardin, Loir-et-Cher

SIGHTS & EVENTS
Château, open June to September;
tel. (0254) 850774.
WHERE TO STAY
Restaurant Cheval Rouge, place Foch,
Montoire; tel. (0254) 850705.
WHERE TO EAT
Restaurant Relais d'Antan, on the Loir;
tel. (0254) 866133.
Restaurant Cheval Rouge (see above).
INFORMATION
16 place Clemenceau, Montoire;
tel. (0254) 852330.

Levroux, Indre

WHERE TO STAY
Hôtel-Restaurant Cloche, 3 rue Nationale;
tel. (0254) 357043.
WHERE TO EAT
Restaurant Relais Saint-Jean,
34 rue Nationale;
tel. (0254) 358156.
Restaurant du Centre, rue Victor-Hugo;
tel. (0254) 356354.
INFORMATION
Maison de Bois; tel. (0254) 356339.

Montrésor, Indre-et-Loire

SIGHTS & EVENTS
Château, open April to September;
tel. (0247) 926004.
Market, Saturday mornings.
WHERE TO STAY
Mme. Willems, *Le Moulin* (guest house);
tel. (0247) 926820.
Mme. Pivet, 15 rue Branicki (guest house);
tel. (0247) 926926.
WHERE TO EAT
Restaurant Relais Agnès Sorel (also has
rooms), 10 km west, at Genille;
tel. (0247) 595017.
Restaurant Auberge des Charmettes (also has
rooms), 3 km north, at Beaumont-Village;
tel. (0247) 927581.
Café de la Ville, 29 Grande-Rue;
tel. (0247) 927531.

The sumptuous apartments of the château of Cheverny (Loir-et-Cher) (opposite).

INFORMATION
23 Grande-Rue; tel. (0247) 914307.

Montrichard, Loir-et-Cher

SIGHTS & EVENTS
Donjon des Aigles; tel. (0254) 320116.
Wine production, Caves Monmousseau;
tel. (0254) 716666.
Markets, Monday & Friday afternoons.
WHERE TO STAY
Hôtel-Restaurant Château de la Menaudière,
2.5 km north-west of Montrichard;
tel. (0254) 712345.
Hôtel-Restaurant La Tête Noire,
24 rue Tours; tel. (0254) 320555.
Hôtel La Croix Blanche,
64 rue Nationale; tel. (0254) 323087.
WHERE TO EAT
See first two entries above.
INFORMATION
1 rue du Pont; tel. (0254) 320510.

Richelieu, Indre-et-Loire

SIGHTS & EVENTS
Steam trains, July & August, at the railway
station; tel. (0247) 581297.
WHERE TO STAY
Mme. Couvrat-Desvernes, 6 rue Henri
Proust (guest house);
tel. (0247) 582940.
Mme. Leplatre, 1 rue Jarry (guest house);
tel. (0247) 581042.
INFORMATION
6 Grande-Rue; tel. (0247) 581362.

Saint-Aignan, Loir-et-Cher

WHERE TO STAY
Hôtel-Restaurant Clos du Cher, 1 km north;
tel. (0254) 750003.
*Hôtel-Restaurant Grand Hôtel de Saint-
Aignan*; tel. (0254) 751804.
Hôtel-Restaurant du Moulin, 7 rue de
Novilliers; tel. (0254) 751554.
WHERE TO EAT
See above.
INFORMATION
26 place Wilson; tel. (0254) 752285

*T he rooftops of Montrésor
(Indre-et-Loire) (opposite).*

Selles-sur-Cher, Loir-et-Cher

SIGHTS & EVENTS
Château, open July to September;
guided tours; tel. (0254) 976398.
WHERE TO STAY
Restaurant Le Lion d'Or, 14 place de la Paix;
tel. (0254) 974083.
WHERE TO EAT
See above.
INFORMATION
Place Charles de Gaulle; tel. (0254) 952544.

Tours, Indre-et-Loire

WHERE TO STAY
Hôtel Mondial, 3 place de la Résistance;
tel. (0247) 056268.
WHERE TO EAT
Restaurant La Ruche, 105 rue Colbert;
tel. (0247) 666983.
INFORMATION
78 rue Bernard-Palissy; tel. (0247) 703737.

Villandry, Indre-et-Loire

SIGHTS & EVENTS
Château, open all year; tel. (0247) 500209.
Goat cheese production, Domaine de la
Giraudière; tel. (0247) 500860.
WHERE TO STAY
Hôtel-Restaurant Le Cheval Rouge;
tel. (0247) 500207.
WHERE TO EAT
See above.
INFORMATION
At the château.

AROUND ANGERS
AND NANTES

Angers, Maine-et-Loire

SIGHTS & EVENTS
Château, open all year; tel. (0241) 874347.
WHERE TO STAY
Hôtel Progrès, 26 rue Docteur Papin;
tel. (0241) 881014.
WHERE TO EAT
Restaurant Lucullus, 5 rue Hoche;
tel. (0241) 870044.

INFORMATION
13 promenade du Bout du Monde;
tel. (0241) 235111.

Baugé, Maine-et-Loire

SIGHTS & EVENTS
Château, tel. (0241) 891807.
Museum at the château, open April to
October; tel. (0241) 891807.
WHERE TO STAY
Hôtel-Restaurant La Boule d'Or,
4 rue Cygne; tel. (0241) 898212.
Hôtel-Restaurant des Voyageurs, 18 rue
Victor-Hugo; tel. (0241) 891206.
Mme. Charrier, *La Prieure* (guest house),
6 km away, at Chartrené;
tel. (0241) 827322.
WHERE TO EAT
See above.
INFORMATION
At the château.

Beaufort-en-Vallée, Maine-et-Loire

SIGHTS & EVENTS
Museum, open April to October, 5 place
Nôtre-Dame; tel. (0241) 574050.
WHERE TO STAY
Hôtel-Restaurant Les Voyageurs, carrefour
Chardavoine; tel. (0241) 572400.
M. et Mme. Lambert, 47 rue du Docteur
Grimoux (guest house);
tel. (0241) 803687.
WHERE TO EAT
Restaurant au P'tit Creux, 6 rue de la
Maladrerie; tel. (0241) 803861.
INFORMATION
Place Joseph-Denais; tel. (0241) 574230.

Chenillé-Changé, Maine-et-Loire

SIGHTS & EVENTS
Water-mill, open March to October;
tel. (0241) 951083.
Boat trips; tel. (0241) 951083.
Château des Rues (also has rooms);
tel. (0241) 951064.
WHERE TO STAY
Château des Rues (see above).

WHERE TO EAT
Restaurant La Table du Meunier;
tel. (0241) 951083.

Clisson, Loire-Atlantique

WHERE TO STAY
Hôtel-Restaurant Gare, place Gare;
tel. (0240) 361655.
WHERE TO EAT
Restaurant Bonne Auberge, 1 rue O. de
Clisson; tel. (0240) 540190.
Restaurant Gétignière, 3 km away,
at Gétigné; tel. (0240) 360537.
INFORMATION
Place de la Trinité; tel. (0240) 540295.

Fontevraud -l'Abbaye, Maine-et-Loire

SIGHTS & EVENTS
Abbey, open all year; tel. (0241) 517141.
Market, Wednesdays.
WHERE TO STAY
Hôtel-Restaurant Prieuré Saint-Lazare,
in the abbey grounds; tel. (0241) 517316.
Hôtel-Restaurant Croix Blanche,
place des Plantagenets;
tel. (0241) 517111.
WHERE TO EAT
Restaurant La Licorne, allée Sainte-
Catherine; tel. (0241) 517249.
Restaurant Abbaye, rue Montsoreau;
tel. (0241) 517104.
INFORMATION
Chapelle Sainte-Catherine;
tel. (0241) 517945.

La Meilleraie, Loire-Atlantique

SIGHTS & EVENTS
Sailing trips, Écomusée de la Loire
Angevine, quai des Mariniers, Montjean;
tel. (0241) 390710.
WHERE TO STAY
Hôtel-Restaurant Hostellerie de la Gabelle,
12 quai de la Loire, Saint-Florent;
tel. (0241) 725019.
Hôtel-Restaurant L'Auberge de la Loire,
2 quai des Mariniers, Montjean;
tel. (0241) 398020.

WHERE TO EAT
See above.
INFORMATION
At Saint-Florent-le-Vieil, place de la
Mairie; tel. (0241) 726232.

Le Lion-d'Angers, Maine-et-Loire

SIGHTS & EVENTS
National stud, Isle-Briand; open all year;
tel. (0241) 958246.
WHERE TO STAY
Hôtel-Restaurant Les Voyageurs, 2 rue du
Général Leclerc; tel. (0241) 958181.
Le Petit Carqueron (guest house),
1.5 km west of Le Lion-d'Angers;
tel. (0241) 956265.
WHERE TO EAT
Restaurant Madona, rue du Canal;
tel. (0241) 956713.
INFORMATION
Square des Villes Jumelées;
tel. (0241) 958319.

Montreuil-Bellay, Maine-et-Loire

SIGHTS & EVENTS
Château, open April to October;
tel. (0241) 523306.
Market, Tuesdays.
WHERE TO STAY
Hôtel-Restaurant Relais du Bellay, 96 rue
Nationale; tel. (0241) 524517.
Hôtel-Restaurant l'Auberge des Isles, 312 rue
du Boelle; tel. (0241) 523063.
Mr. & Mrs. Smith, *La Maison Aubelle*
(guest house); tel. (0241) 523639.
WHERE TO EAT
Restaurant Hostellerie Saint-Jean, 432 rue
Nationale; tel. (0241) 523041.
INFORMATION
Place de la Concorde; tel. (0241) 523239.

Nantes, Loire-Atlantique

SIGHTS & EVENTS
Château, open all year; tel. (0240) 415656.
WHERE TO STAY
Hôtel Amiral, 26 bis, rue Scribe;
tel. (0240) 692021.

WHERE TO EAT
Restaurant La Cigale, 4 place Graslin;
tel. (0251) 849494.
INFORMATION
Place du Commerce; tel. (0240) 206000.

Oudon, Loire-Atlantique

SIGHTS & EVENTS
Château, opening hours from the Mairie;
tel. (0240) 836017.
WHERE TO STAY
L'Hôtel du Port (restaurant with rooms),
10 place du Port; tel. (0240) 836858.
WHERE TO EAT
Restaurant Le Malestroit, rue de la Gare;
tel. (0240) 838319.
INFORMATION
Rue du Pont-Levis; tel. (0240) 838004.

*A corner of the beautifully
restored monastic complex of
Fontevraud-l'Abbaye (Maine-et-
Loire).*

Saint-Fiacre-sur-Maine, Loire-Atlantique

SIGHTS & EVENTS
Wine production, Mme. Günther-Chereau, Château du Coing;
tel. (0240) 548524.
WHERE TO STAY
Château Pléssis-Brezot (guest house),
Pléssis-Brezot, nr. Monnières;
tel. (0240) 546324.
WHERE TO EAT
Restaurant Monte-Cristo, 8 km north-west,
at Vertou; tel. (0240) 344036.
INFORMATION
Place du Beau Verger, Vertou;
tel. (0240) 341222.

Saumur, Maine-et-Loire

SIGHTS & EVENTS
Château, open all year; tel. (0241) 402440.
WHERE TO STAY
Hôtel Saint-Pierre, place Saint-Pierre;
tel. (0241) 512625.
WHERE TO EAT
Restaurant Délices du Château, cour du
Château; tel. (0241) 676560.
INFORMATION
Place de la Bilange; tel. (0241) 402060.

Savennières, Maine-et-Loire

SIGHTS & EVENTS
Wine production, Mmes. de Jessey,
Domaine du Closel; tel. (0241) 728100.

WHERE TO STAY
Mme. Marchesi, 3 place du Mail (guest
house); tel. (0241) 722810.
Mme. Charpentier (guest house),
2 km west; tel. (0241) 391321.
INFORMATION
1 rue de la Mairie; tel. (0241) 728446.

Sucé-sur-Erdre, Loire-Atlantique

WHERE TO STAY
Hôtel-Restaurant Au Cordon Bleu;
tel. (0240) 777134.
WHERE TO EAT
Restaurant Chataignerie, 156 route
Carquefou; tel. (0240) 779095.
Restaurant La Brigantine, 88 rue de la
Mairie; tel. (0240) 777717.
INFORMATION
Quai de Cricklade;
tel. (0240) 777066.

Trentemoult, Loire-Atlantique

WHERE TO STAY
Hôtel Cheval Blanc, 2 km east, at Rezé;
tel. (0240) 756507.
WHERE TO EAT
Restaurant Les Goelands,
13 quai Michel Boissard;
tel. (0240) 758440.
INFORMATION
At Nantes; tel. (0240) 206000.

Further Reading

BARBOUR, PHILIPPE, *The Loire,* London, 1997
— *Lazy Days Out in the Loire,* London, 1997
BENTLEY, JAMES with WAITE, CHARLIE, *The Loire,* London, 1981
GOUVION, COLETTE, *Châteaux of the Loire,* London, 1986
JAMES, HENRY, *A Little Tour in France,* (re-issue) London, 1985
WALDEN, HILAIRE, *Loire Gastronomique,* New York, 1993
WARNER, MARINA, *Joan of Arc,* New York, 1991